THE MURDER OF LACI PETERSON

By Carla Mooney

AMERICAN CRIME STORIES

Essential Library

An Imprint of Abdo Publishing | abdobooks.com

ABDOBOOKS.COM

Published by Abdo Publishing, a division of ABDO, PO Box 398166, Minneapolis, Minnesota 55439.

Printed in the United States of America, North Mankato, Minnesota.
102023
012024

THIS BOOK CONTAINS
RECYCLED MATERIALS

Cover Photos: Bart Ah You/Getty Images News/Getty Images (Scott Peterson); Justin Sullivan/Getty Images News/Getty Images (poster)
Interior Photos: Paul Sakuma/AP Images, 5, 35, 47, 68–69; Red Line Editorial, 7, 57; iStockphoto, 8; Justin Sullivan/Getty Images News/Getty Images, 10, 38; Al Golub/Getty Images News/Getty Images, 13, 19, 65, 74; David Paul Morris/Getty Images News/Getty Images, 14–15, 55, 79; Monica M. Davey/Getty Images News/Getty Images, 16; Ben Margot/AP Images, 23; Michael Macor/San Francisco Chronicle/Hearst Newspapers/Getty Images, 27; Debbie Noda/Modesto Bee/Tribune News Service/Getty Images, 29; Ann Johansson/AP Images, 33; Modesto Police Department/Getty Images News/Getty Images, 37; Mitch Gerber/starmaxinc.com/AP Images, 41; Paul Chinn/San Francisco Chronicle/Hearst Newspapers/Getty Images, 45, 92; Julie Jacobson/AP Images, 46; Paul Sakuma/Getty Images News/Getty Images, 50; Cindi Christie/Contra Costa Times/KRT/Abaca Press/Alamy, 53; Stanislaus County Sheriff's Office/Getty Images News/Getty Images, 61; Bart Ah You/Modesto Bee/AP Images, 77; Lou Dematteis/AFP/Getty Images, 82; Monica Davey/Getty Images News/Getty Images, 84; California Department of Corrections and Rehabilitation/AP Images, 89; Jeff Chiu/AP Images, 97

Editor: Christa Kelly
Series Designer: Melissa Martin

Library of Congress Control Number: 2023939441

PUBLISHER'S CATALOGING-IN-PUBLICATION DATA

Names: Mooney, Carla, author.
Title: The murder of Laci Peterson / by Carla Mooney
Description: Minneapolis, Minnesota: Abdo Publishing, 2024 | Series: American crime stories | Includes online resources and index.
Identifiers: ISBN 9781098292133 (lib. bdg.) | ISBN 9798384910077 (ebook)
Subjects: LCSH: Crime and criminals--Juvenile literature. | Killing (Murder)--Juvenile literature. | United States--Juvenile literature. | Peterson, Laci--Juvenile literature. | Peterson, Scott, 1972- --Juvenile literature. | California--Modesto--Juvenile literature. | Murderers--Juvenile literature.
Classification: DDC 364.97--dc23

CONTENTS

This book discusses accounts of crime, violence, and death that may be disturbing to some readers.

CHAPTER ONE

MISSING

On December 24, 2002, Sharon Rocha's phone rang. It was Christmas Eve, and Rocha was preparing for a family dinner at her quiet home in central California. She answered the phone; it was her son-in-law, 30-year-old Scott Peterson. Scott asked if Laci, his wife and Rocha's 27-year-old daughter, was already at her house.

"No," she told him. Rocha had not seen Laci that day.

"Laci's car is at the house, and McKenzie [the Petersons' dog] is in the backyard with his leash on. Laci is missing," Scott said.[1]

For a moment, Rocha was confused. Missing? Her daughter was eight months pregnant and always prompt. She was supposed to be arriving with Scott shortly for a holiday dinner. How could she be missing? Then, fear gripped Rocha. She worried Laci had gone into labor and been rushed to the hospital. She told Scott to call the couple's friends and neighbors to see if anyone had heard from Laci.

Laci and Scott Peterson had been married for five years when Laci went missing.

LACI
LACI'S

> ### THE CITY OF MODESTO
>
> Modesto is a city in central California. It is about 1.5 hours southeast of Sacramento, two hours southeast of San Francisco, and two hours northeast of San Jose. Modesto is part of the San Joaquin Valley, an agricultural region where dairy, nuts, fruits, wine grapes, and poultry products are produced.[2]

When she hung up the phone, Rocha turned to her longtime partner, Ron Grantski. She told him that Scott had said Laci was missing. A few minutes later, the phone rang again. It was Scott. He said no one had seen Laci. Scott also told Rocha that Laci had planned to walk their dog that morning. Her usual walking route went through East La Loma Park, the park at the end of their street. But the dog was at home, while Laci was not. Rocha told Scott to meet her at the park. Then she hung up, called her friend Sandy Rickard, and asked for help finding Laci. As the two women left for the park, Rocha turned to her husband and told him to call the police.

Reported Missing

Approximately 30 minutes after Scott's first call, Grantski called 911 to report Laci missing. Usually, the police wait at least 24 hours to respond to a missing person report for an adult. However, the police were concerned because Laci was eight months pregnant. They worried that she was experiencing a medical problem because of her pregnancy

MODESTO, CALIFORNIA

In 2000, Modesto, California, had a population of approximately 188,256 people.[3]

In 2002, the year Laci went missing, Modesto's violent crime rate was significantly higher than the national average.

or had been injured. By 6:00 p.m., officers from the Modesto Police Department headed to East La Loma Park and the Petersons' home.

Jon Evers, a 16-year veteran of the Modesto Police Department, was the first officer to arrive at the park. Rocha and several family members, including Scott, were already there. Evers questioned Scott about when he had last seen his wife. Scott told Evers that he had left their home around 9:30 a.m. to go fishing. According to Scott, Laci was mopping the kitchen floor when he left, and she planned to take their dog for a walk in the park later that morning. After that, she planned to get groceries and bake cookies before dinner at her mother's house. Scott said that when he returned home that afternoon, he found the dog in the backyard with his leash still attached. Laci was not home.

At the Peterson Home

Evers went to the Petersons' home to examine the scene. The couple lived in a one-story ranch house on Covena Avenue. It was a modest, friendly neighborhood. Evers and the other officers set up a command center for the missing person case at the Petersons' house.

Officers examined the Peterson home. They entered through the front door, which was unlocked. They walked through the living room, kitchen, and nursery. They opened closet doors and looked in bathrooms, searching for anything unusual. Officer Evers asked Scott to walk through the house with them to see if he noticed anything out of place. They found Laci's purse in her closet, with her wallet, keys, and other personal items still inside.

As they moved from room to room, Evers again asked Scott about his day. This time, Scott pulled a piece of paper from his pocket to show a receipt from Berkeley Marina to prove where he had been that afternoon. Evers exchanged a glance with Officer Matt Spurlock. They thought it was odd that Scott was so quick to hand over proof of his whereabouts without being asked.

The officers asked Scott about his fishing trip, but his answers were vague and awkward. He said he had called Laci on his way home and had left a voice mail when she did not answer. Then Scott recounted his steps when he got home.

When he arrived at the house around 4:30 p.m., he noticed Laci's car was in the driveway and their dog was in the backyard with its leash still attached. When Scott went inside, the house was dark, and there was no sign of Laci. He said he assumed Laci had gone to her mother's home early. After grabbing some pizza from the refrigerator, Scott took a shower and washed his clothes, explaining they were wet and dirty from fishing. It was after 5:00 p.m. when he finally called his in-laws and learned Laci was not there. At that point, Scott said, he began to worry about his wife.

As hours passed, search efforts for Laci Peterson increased. The Stanislaus County Sheriff's Office sent its helicopters to fly over the park looking for the pregnant woman. On the ground, the Modesto police brought in a search dog to check different areas throughout the park. Numerous people searched the park and the surrounding area. The police checked local hospitals,

More than 2,200 volunteers joined the search for Laci Peterson.

and patrol units searched the neighborhood, but no trace of Laci was found.

Doubts Arise

Officer Byron Duerfeldt called his supervisor, Sergeant Alan Carter, and reported that the officers at the scene were uncomfortable with Scott's answers. Carter called Detective Al Brocchini and sent him to the Petersons' home. Brocchini was part of Stanislaus County's Crimes Against Persons (CAP) Unit, which specialized in felony crimes, including suspicious deaths and homicides. It had been less than an hour since Laci's stepfather had called 911, but Carter wanted a homicide detective there as soon as possible.

At the Peterson home, Brocchini approached Scott and asked him to walk through the house with him. He asked Scott detailed questions about his movements that day. He examined Scott's pickup truck. Together, they drove to Scott's workplace, a warehouse four miles (6 km) away.[4] Scott was a fertilizer salesman who serviced customers in California, Arizona, and

CRIMES AGAINST PERSONS (CAP) UNIT

Officers from the Crimes Against Persons (CAP) Unit responded to the missing person call about Laci Peterson. The unit included six full-time detectives who investigated cases that involved felony assault, robbery, homicide, and missing persons. On December 24, 2002, the day that Laci Peterson was reported missing, Sergeant Alan Carter was the head of the Stanislaus County CAP Unit.[5]

New Mexico. At the warehouse, detectives inspected the boat that Scott had taken fishing earlier in the day.

After searching the warehouse, Brocchini and Evers drove Scott to the Modesto police headquarters for a formal interview. The taped interview lasted until 1:30 a.m., and it wasn't until after 4:00 a.m. on Christmas morning that Scott finally returned home. Yellow police tape surrounded the empty house. Meanwhile, detectives were growing increasingly sure that Laci's disappearance was suspicious. They could not shake the feeling that Scott was involved.

"I had a gut feeling, and the patrol officers out there had gut feelings," says Detective Brocchini. "[Scott] went fishing 90 miles [145 km] from home on Christmas Eve with an 8.5-month pregnant wife. When we questioned him a couple of hours after he got home, he didn't know what he was fishing for or what bait he was using. Those were red flags."[6]

GOLF OR FISHING?

Scott Peterson told detectives that he had been fishing when his wife vanished. However, others say he told them a different story. Harvey Kemple, who is married to Sharon Rocha's cousin, talked to Scott on the night of December 24. Kemple testified in court that Scott told him that he was not with Laci that day because he had been playing golf. Two neighbors of the Petersons also testified that Scott told them that night that he had been golfing earlier in the day.

At the end of Scott's formal interview, police tested his hands for gunpowder residue after finding a gun in Scott's truck.

CHAPTER TWO

SCOTT AND LACI

On May 4, 1975, Sharon and Dennis Rocha welcomed their daughter, Laci Denise Rocha, to the world. According to her parents, Laci was a happy child. She loved being outside and especially enjoyed learning about plants and helping her mother in the garden. She began helping with the family dairy farm at a young age, pulling on rubber boots to wade through the everyday muck of farm life.

"It was a great place to grow up," said Laci's brother, Brent Rocha. "We always had a good time out

Sharon Rocha met her longtime partner Ron Grantski when Laci was two years old. He was described as being like a father to Laci.

Scott was the only child Lee and Jackie Peterson had together. Jackie passed away in 2013.

there. As a kid on a dairy [farm], you kind of have to make your own fun."[1]

When her parents divorced, Laci and her brother moved to Modesto with their mother. They visited their father at the dairy farm on weekends. Laci and Brent grew close as they learned to navigate life with divorced parents.

As a teenager, Laci went to Downey High School in Modesto. She had a close circle of friends who had grown up together in elementary and junior high school. Laci's bright smile and engaging personality made her the center of attention wherever she went.

After graduating high school in 1993, Laci enrolled in California Polytechnic State University (Cal Poly) in San Luis Obispo, California. She studied ornamental horticulture and earned the outstanding freshman award. While in college, she often visited a restaurant called the Pacific Café, where she knew one of the workers. There, she met a young server named Scott Peterson.

Scott's Early Life

Scott Peterson was born in San Diego, California, on October 24, 1972. His parents, Lee and Jackie Peterson, each had three children from previous relationships. Scott was the baby of his blended family, and everyone doted on him. When Scott was little, Lee worked for a trucking company, and Jackie owned a small dress shop. She often brought Scott to work with her and helped customers as he watched from a crib. Because Jackie's father had been killed when she was young, she worked hard to give Scott and his siblings the life she never had. The family often joked that Scott's feet never touched the floor because so many older half siblings were around to carry him.

When Scott was four years old, the Peterson family bought a home in Scripps Ranch, a San Diego suburb. Around this time, Lee started a shipping and packing business. He often took Scott with him as he drove through the city to pick up packages. Lee taught his children some of his favorite pastimes, such as golfing, fishing, and hunting pheasants. Family pictures show a young Scott gripping a golf club and ball or proudly holding a fish he caught.

Professional golfer Phil Mickelson and Scott Peterson played together on the same high school golf team.

As a teen, Scott worked part-time at a country club in Rancho Santa Fe, picking up golf balls and filling golf carts with gas. As an employee, he was given free golf lessons and playing privileges at the club. By the time he was 14 years old, Scott could outshoot his father on the golf course.

A talented golfer, Scott enrolled in the University of San Diego High School, a college preparatory school with a good golf program. Scott played for the school's varsity golf team from 1987 to 1990. He was awarded the team's most valuable player award twice and named to the *San Diego Union-Tribune*'s All-Academic Team for three years. His coach, David Thoennes, remembers Scott as being polite and controlled.

"He was very respectful," Thoennes says. "I don't think I ever heard Scott use foul language. Some kids will hit a bad shot and go into all kinds of antics. Scott would hit a bad shot and go to the next one. I don't think I ever saw him get out of control."[2]

After high school, Scott attended Arizona State University and tried out for the golf team. There is no record of him on the school's golf roster, and he left the university after one semester. He moved in with his parents in a cottage in Morro Bay, California, and switched to a junior college. Scott attended Cuesta College in San Luis Obispo from the spring of 1992 to

One of Scott's golf teammates later described him as a snob.

the spring of 1993 and played on the school's golf team. When he was 20, Scott announced to his parents that he was moving out and no longer needed their financial support.

"I've had the greatest parents," he told them. "You don't owe me anything."[3] He moved into an apartment that he shared with his golf teammates. The roommates covered the garage's flat roof with artificial grass and used it as a driving range to hit golf balls into a nearby pasture.

In 1994, Scott transferred to Cal Poly. He majored in agricultural business and worked three jobs—as a waiter and at two golf courses—to pay his expenses. Professors described Scott as a pleasure to have in class.

"He seemed more mature than most," recalled Jim Ahern, an agribusiness professor at Scott's school. "He was pleasant to deal with. I wouldn't mind having a class full of Scott Petersons."[4]

A Chance Meeting

In 1995, while Scott was working a shift at the Pacific Café, a young woman caught his attention. She was Laci Rocha, a fellow Cal Poly student, and Scott was quickly interested in her. The feeling was mutual. Laci asked a friend who worked at the Pacific Café to give her phone number to Scott. Later, she told her mother that she'd met the man she would marry, even if they had not yet had a first date. Laci was confident that Scott would call her. She was right. Their first date was a deep-sea fishing trip. Laci's mother met Scott the next weekend. He brought two bouquets of roses, one for each woman. Scott seemed to be the perfect gentleman.

WILLIAM "KENT" GAIN

When Laci in high school, she met an older boy named William "Kent" Gain, and the two teenagers began dating. Though Sharon Rocha and Ron Grantski initially liked Gain, they became concerned about his temper and lack of respect. Laci and Gain broke up during Laci's freshman year of college. Years later, Gain was charged with attempted murder after shooting his girlfriend. He was sentenced to 15 years in prison. After hearing about Laci's disappearance, Gain professed to still love Laci.

Laci did not know, however, that as her relationship with Scott was beginning, he was still begging his ex-girlfriend Lauren Putnant to get back together with him. Scott and Lauren had broken up a few weeks before Scott and Laci's first date, and Scott even brought Laci to the restaurant where Lauren worked to make Lauren jealous. Approximately two months after their breakup, Lauren moved out of San Luis Obispo and never spoke to Scott again.

Getting Serious

By Christmas 1995, Laci had moved into Scott's apartment. Laci's Christmas gift to Scott that year was a puppy they named McKenzie. In the spring of 1996, Laci graduated from Cal Poly with a degree in ornamental horticulture.

On August 9, 1997, Scott and Laci were married in an elegant ceremony at the Sycamore Mineral Springs Resort in San Luis Obispo. The wedding day was beautiful and sunny, and Laci walked down the aisle in a sleeveless wedding dress and a flowing white veil. During the reception, Scott toasted his new in-laws and thanked them for their "perfect daughter."[5] Yet despite the picture-perfect day, investigators would later learn some troubling details about the event. The resort's general manager told police that Scott was drinking at the bar before the wedding ceremony and inappropriately flirting with one of the servers.

After the wedding, the couple briefly lived apart. Laci worked in Prunedale, California, while Scott finished his college degree 130 miles (209 km) away.[6] The distance allowed Scott to date at least two other women without his wife's knowledge.

One of those women, Katy Hansen, was also a Cal Poly student. Katy and Scott dated for about two and a half months, and he never told her he was married. On his June 1998 graduation day, Katy sat beside Scott and was stunned when Scott introduced Laci to her as his wife. In shock, Katy did not ask questions; she did not talk to Scott again and was thankful their relationship had not gotten more serious.

JANET ILSE

Shortly after Scott and Laci married, Scott started dating a Cal Poly sophomore named Janet Ilse who did not know he was married. At the time, Scott was finishing his college degree and living off campus with three male roommates while Laci worked in Prunedale. One night, Ilse arrived at Scott's apartment and one of his roommates let her in. She walked into Scott's bedroom and found him with Laci. Ilse yelled at Scott before storming out. That was the end of their relationship.

Restaurant Business

After Scott's graduation, he and Laci worked hard to convert an empty storefront in a strip mall into a restaurant they named The Shack. Located near the Cal Poly campus, The Shack served beer, wine, and sandwiches, and Scott used what he had learned as a waiter to get the restaurant up and running. The Shack was a casual hangout that became popular with local college students.

However, after about two years, Scott and Laci grew disenchanted with the restaurant business. It was challenging to find reliable employees. And they had to be on call 24-7, with employees constantly calling with problems when the couple had a day off work. In 2000, they sold the restaurant to a new owner.

Move to Modesto

After selling The Shack, the couple moved closer to Laci's parents in Modesto. Real estate was cheaper in that part of California, and Laci still had many high school friends in

Laci and Scott purchased their Modesto home for $177,000.

the area. It was a place they could raise a family. Using money from Scott's parents, the couple purchased a house on Covena Avenue in October 2000. Scott and Laci spent a lot of time fixing up their home. They painted and tiled bathrooms, planted flowers, and built a brick wall in the yard. They also borrowed money to add a swimming pool in the backyard.

Scott took a new sales job with Tradecorp, an agricultural supply company based in Spain. Tradecorp was trying to expand into the United States and hired Scott as its West Coast representative to sell irrigation systems, fertilizers, plant nutrients, and other agricultural products. In his role, Scott frequently traveled to visit his customers, most of whom were big farmers and flower growers located in the region. He typically spent at least one night a week away from home.

In Modesto, the couple kept a full social calendar. Laci took a part-time job as a substitute teacher, while Scott joined the local country club to play golf and became the youngest member of Modesto's Rotary Club. They hosted dinner parties and entertained friends and family at their new home. Often, they served fancy foods and expensive wines. Laci insisted that guests dress for dinner and not be late. "Laci wanted to be sure, each and every time we were all together, that we would have fun," said one friend. "Laci not only taught us proper etiquette, but how to laugh. And not just giggle, but to laugh loud and often."[7]

Baby on the Way

Settled into their new home, Scott and Laci began trying to have a baby. For two years, they were unsuccessful, and Laci wondered if she should see a fertility specialist. However, before she could see a doctor, Laci discovered she was pregnant. She was thrilled, and Scott appeared to be just as excited about the new baby. "I assume if he didn't want to have a child, he wouldn't have allowed it to happen," said Sharon Rocha.[8]

Scott and Laci went to classes to prepare for their baby boy's birth, and Laci took a prenatal yoga class. They decorated their nursery with a nautical theme, complete with a model boat made by Lee Peterson and a life raft on the wall. They named their unborn son Conner. Even after Laci entered her third trimester, she took walks with their dog around the neighborhood. To those who knew them, Scott and Laci's life appeared to be perfect.

SECOND THOUGHTS

Not everyone remembers Scott Peterson being excited about becoming a father. In 2001, Rosemarie Rocha, Laci's sister-in-law, had a troubling conversation with Scott. He told Rocha that he was partially hoping that he and Laci would be infertile and unable to have children. Later, when Laci announced her pregnancy in 2002, Rocha assumed that Scott had gotten over his reservations about having a child because he went to doctor's appointments with Laci and appeared enthusiastic.

CHAPTER THREE

A MASSIVE SEARCH

On Christmas morning 2002, Laci's disappearance was front-page news. The search for the missing pregnant woman was growing by the minute. More than two dozen police officers searched her neighborhood, knocking on doors in hopes of talking to someone who had information about where Laci could be.

Detective Jon Buehler was one of the officers gathering information from Laci and Scott's neighbors. One neighbor had heard a dog barking at about 10:30 a.m., while another doubted Laci would have been walking the dog that morning because her pregnancy made her too tired. Karen Servas lived next door to the Petersons. She had found their dog, McKenzie, on the street and took him home. Because the front gate was locked, Servas entered through the Petersons' back gate by

Over the course of the search for Laci, thousands of flyers were distributed.

S&S
RENTAL UNIT
BOAT
MISSING
$500,000 REWARD
Laci (Rocha) Peterson
27 years old
Height 5'1"
Weight 140 lbs
Eight Months Pregnant
Brown Eyes
Brown Hair
Last seen 12/24 at 9:30 am. She was seen in Modesto near Dry Creek in the La Loma area walking her Golden Retriever. Wearing white long sleeve shirt & black pants.
line at (209) 342-6166.
GUARANTEED

QUESTIONING SEX OFFENDERS

In the search for Laci, police officers questioned hundreds of local sex offenders and parolees. One potential suspect confessed to the crime, saying that he had murdered a woman named Lisa Peterson and the only witness to the crime was her dog. However, the man's confession was dismissed because he had mental health problems.

the pool and left the dog in the yard. None of the neighbors believed there was any trouble in the Petersons' marriage.

Calling In Homicide

At approximately 11:30 a.m. on Christmas Day, Brocchini called Detective Craig Grogan and requested that the Homicide Division become involved in the case. Grogan joined Detective Buehler at the police station. Scott Peterson had agreed the day before to take a polygraph test. The polygraph was scheduled for that afternoon. However, as Grogan and Buehler talked, Buehler received a phone call. Scott Peterson had decided not to take the polygraph test and said his father had advised him against it.

"When somebody's in a position like him, and they didn't do it, usually they'll say, 'Take blood, take a polygraph, I don't care,'" said Detective Buehler. "But Scott wouldn't do that. He'd only go to a point."[1]

The detectives met Scott at police headquarters and asked him for an additional interview, and Scott agreed, telling

Grogan that he wanted to help. The detectives asked Scott about his background with Laci, how they had met, and about their life together. They asked him to describe the days leading up to Laci's disappearance. Then they asked him to once again go over the details of December 24.

Interviewing Scott

Scott told investigators that when he got up on Christmas Eve morning at about 8:00 a.m., Laci was already awake and preparing food for the next day's Christmas brunch. Scott said Laci was wearing a plain white shirt and black maternity pants. Scott also said that Laci was wearing some valuable diamond jewelry, which she had inherited from her

Scott's attitude made investigators suspicious. They said he seemed too calm and unconcerned about Laci.

late grandmother. He again said she planned to walk the dog, go grocery shopping, and bake gingerbread that afternoon. Scott described Laci's regular walking routine and route, noting that it usually took 45 minutes. He said she always took the dog with her.

After breakfast, Scott decided to go fishing in the boat he'd bought two weeks earlier. He told detectives that he left home at approximately 9:30 a.m. Although Scott had been vague about his fishing plans with officers the day before, he was very detailed with his account this time. He told Grogan that he'd fished for sturgeon and stripers.

Scott first drove his truck to his warehouse and sent a few emails. He then assembled a woodworking tool, cleaned up his office, unloaded tools from his toolbox, and hooked up his boat to the truck. A little after 11:00 a.m., he left the warehouse and drove to Berkeley Marina. Scott arrived at the marina at approximately 1:00 p.m. and collected a timed parking receipt. He loaded two fishing rods and a tackle box into the boat but forgot the new lures he had bought a few days earlier.

Scott said he drove the boat around San Francisco Bay for about an hour. He motored northwest and did a little fishing. When it began to rain, he returned to the marina. On his way home, at approximately 2:15 p.m., he called Laci. When she did not answer the home phone, he left her a voice mail and left another message on her cell phone.

NEIGHBORHOOD ROBBERY

Around the time Laci Peterson disappeared, one of her neighbors' homes was robbed. The neighbors left town on December 24, 2002. When they returned on December 26, they discovered the door to their home had been kicked in and several items, including money, two guns, and a locked safe, had been stolen. At first, police wondered if the robbery was connected to Laci's disappearance. However, police later caught the two burglars and cleared them of any involvement in the Peterson case.

Driving back to the warehouse, Scott got stuck in traffic and called Laci again, but she did not answer. He got to the warehouse at about 4:30 p.m., quickly unloaded the boat, and headed home. When Scott arrived home, he found his dog in the backyard, still wearing its leash. Scott insisted he thought nothing was strange at the empty house. Instead of looking for his pregnant wife, he ate pizza, washed his clothes, and showered before calling his in-laws.

When asked what he believed had happened to his wife, Scott told the detectives he thought Laci had been attacked in the park during her morning walk. He speculated that her expensive jewelry made her a target for thieves. Laci had been concerned about reports of attacks in the park and mentioned considering bringing pepper spray with her. However, she never did.

After the interview with Scott ended, Grogan huddled with Brocchini and Buehler to compare notes. As they reviewed

Less than 24 hours after his wife was reported missing, Scott Peterson asked the police if they had used cadaver dogs in the search for Laci.

what Scott had told each of them over the past two days, the detectives noted several instances where Scott's story was inconsistent. The detectives also had a gut feeling that something was off about Scott. Buehler explained the behavior that made himself and other detectives suspicious:

> *We've been doing homicides for a while. When you compare Scott's demeanor with other people we've dealt with, he didn't even register on the scale as far as seeming concerned [about Laci]. And when Al played the tape of that lame-o message that Scott left on Laci's phone—"Hey, beautiful, I'm on my way back from fishing. Pick up the basket at Vella Farms. I love you, sweetie," or words to that effect—it just seemed so insincere and false, like he was making this call to make us think he was in love with her. But anybody who has been married for five years knows there aren't too many people who talk to their spouse like that after that amount of time. It didn't mean that he did it; it just meant we needed to work him a little bit closer and clear him.*[2]

Brocchini also told the other men that the boat patrol officer at the marina had said there was no rain on Christmas Eve, directly contradicting Scott's account of the day. Suspicions grew, and the men agreed it was time to look more closely at Scott. Grogan prepared search warrants for the Petersons' home and vehicles, along with Scott's business and boat. The detectives planned to serve the warrants the next day.

Volunteer Efforts

Within 24 hours of Laci's disappearance, her family and friends set up a command center at the nearby Red Lion Hotel to help police as they searched for the missing woman. They printed thousands of flyers with Laci's picture and offered a $100,000 reward for information leading to her safe return.[3] By December 28, the reward rose to $500,000.[4] Hundreds of volunteers fanned out on the Modesto streets, passing out flyers and searching for any clues about Laci's whereabouts.

In those first few days, Sharon Rocha, Ron Grantski, Jackie Peterson, and Lee Peterson appeared in front of news cameras pleading for Laci's return. In an interview with CNN, Lee Peterson begged anyone involved in Laci's disappearance to bring her home safely. "Get her back to us," Lee Peterson said,

Volunteers gathered in East La Loma Park, the Red Lion Hotel, the Petersons' home, and the Doubletree Hotel, *pictured*, to help in the search for Laci.

"and do the right thing. Let's return this woman to her family where she belongs."[5] Sharon Rocha was emotional as she pleaded for her daughter's return. "Whoever has her, please, please, please let her go. Bring her back to us."[6]

Scott noticeably stayed in the background during many of the press conferences. He did not make impassioned pleas for his wife's safe return as other family members did. Instead, Scott declined requests for television appearances and said he wanted the focus to stay on Laci, not him. Many people thought his behavior was unusual for a husband supposedly worried sick about his missing wife. His parents tried to explain his behavior away.

"He's brave, but he's just devastated," said Lee Peterson. "He just would not be a good spokesperson," added Jackie Peterson.[7] But questions remained about Scott's behavior.

Searching for Laci

In the hours after her disappearance, police continued to search for Laci. They conducted searches by air and on the ground. Police and volunteers searched East La Loma Park and the nearby area on foot and horseback. Modesto fire officials used rafts to search Dry Creek, which runs through the park.

Police also brought in canine units to track Laci's scent. However, when the dogs picked up Laci's scent outside her home, they ran down the middle of the street to follow the trail

Investigators collected numerous pieces of potential evidence from the Petersons' home, including a bloodstained comforter, shotgun shells, and a camera. However, investigators were unable to tie any of the items to Laci's murder.

instead of tracking the scent on the sidewalk. The dogs' handler explained that when tracking Laci, the dogs "ran in a manner consistent with a vehicle trail as opposed to a trail left by a person that was walking."[8] The handler believed Laci left her house in a vehicle, not on foot.

Looking for Evidence

Detectives and the Federal Bureau of Investigation (FBI) forensic search team scoured the Petersons' home and property for evidence of what had happened to Laci. They took samples of suspicious stains, vacuumed using special debris-collecting equipment, and collected numerous items, including laptops and handwritten notes, for testing.

On December 26, Detective Brocchini reexamined Scott's truck. He noted that several items he had noticed in the truck on Christmas Eve were missing. Scott appeared to have removed a tan camouflage jacket, a bag with two fishing lures, several backyard umbrellas wrapped in a blue tarp, and a crumpled tan tarp from his truck before police served the search warrant.

On December 27, Detective Brocchini returned to Scott's warehouse. On Christmas Eve, Scott had told him the warehouse had no working electricity. Yet when Brocchini arrived three days later, officers on site showed him two light switches that turned on overhead lights and illuminated the warehouse's interior. "I found it highly suspicious that Scott Peterson would not want me to have the lights on in the business when I was there inspecting his boat," Brocchini said.[9]

At the warehouse, detectives found fresh, dry ready-mix concrete and evidence that someone had been using it to make anchors. "It appeared adding ready-mix to the water made these anchors," Brocchini noted. "After the cement mold set, they were moved from the pitcher and set on the flatbed trailer.

Scott told investigators he used the rest of the concrete to fix his driveway.

From the distinct circles on the trailer, it appeared at least four anchors were made. We could only find the one anchor that was inside the boat."[10]

While searching the warehouse, detectives also found the missing tan camouflage jacket and fishing lures. It was obvious to Brocchini that Scott had returned there after Laci had been reported missing on Christmas Eve, and he wondered what else Scott had hidden.

Detectives brought in a cadaver dog to examine the warehouse more closely. Inside the building, the dog alerted officers to the scent of human remains in several places. The dog detected the scent next to the boat, by several milk crates that held supplies, and on the right side of the boat.

When investigators searched Scott's boat, they found a hair that they believe belonged to Laci.

Defense attorneys later argued that the cadaver dogs that searched the pier and Scott's warehouse were unreliable and may have been confused by other smells.

On December 28, the police arranged for a search of the marina and the Brooks Island area of San Francisco Bay. Three patrol boats, a dive team, a helicopter, and two cadaver dogs arrived that morning. The patrol boats searched 40 miles (64 km) of nearby shoreline but turned up nothing.[11] The cadaver dogs, however, had some interesting reactions at the marina. One of the dogs appeared to react to Laci's scent as it ran through the parking lot and down the boat ramp.

A Phone Call

After days of searching, police were still unable to find any sign of Laci Peterson. Detective Grogan's suspicions grew by the day. Yet, the police still had no hard evidence to link a suspect to the woman's disappearance. Then, late in the afternoon on December 30, Grogan was called to a special invitation-only meeting at police headquarters. Only the officers closest to the Peterson investigation were asked to attend. The topic was a phone call that had come in on the tip line from a woman claiming to be Scott Peterson's girlfriend.

CADAVER DOGS

Cadaver dogs are specially trained to detect the scent of human remains, even when the remains are buried or underwater. Often, cadaver dogs and their human handlers work side by side with law enforcement to find missing persons.

CHAPTER FOUR

SUSPICIONS RISE

On November 20, 2002, Amber Frey, a 27-year-old massage therapist from Fresno, California, met a handsome young man named Scott Peterson through a mutual friend. Scott told Amber that he was not married. "He was good-looking, he was nice, he was funny and attentive to me. All the things any woman would want," says Frey.[1] She would later discover that almost everything Scott told her was a lie.

An Attentive Boyfriend

On their first date, Scott and Frey sang karaoke, slow-danced, and spent the night together in Scott's hotel room. According to Frey, Scott did not wear a wedding ring. He was romantic, pouring champagne for her and putting a strawberry in her glass. The following day, he gave her his cell phone number.

Amber Frey was eliminated as a suspect after she took a lie detector test.

MATCHMAKER

At a trade show at the Disneyland Hotel in October 2002, Scott met a woman named Shawn Sibley for the first time. The two had dinner with two of Scott's acquaintances. According to the other dinner attendees, the conversation quickly turned uncomfortable, with Scott and Sibley discussing sex. Scott and Sibley exchanged phone numbers, and several weeks later, Sibley set up Scott on a blind date with her friend Amber Frey.

Frey, a single mother with a 22-month-old daughter, was quickly attracted to Scott. On their second date, the couple went hiking, and he gave her daughter a children's book. They dined on seafood lasagna and wine before spending the night together again. "He made the comment that there would be many more corks . . . many more bottles to share," Frey says.[2]

The next day, December 3, 2002, Frey asked Scott to pick up her daughter from day care. He appeared happy to do so and met Frey at her home. The three of them went out that night to buy a Christmas tree. While decorating the tree, Scott told Frey that he was never close to having children with anyone.

"Lost His Wife"

The next time Frey saw Scott, on December 9, he confessed that he had lied to her about never being married. He cried and told Frey that he had "lost his wife." Frey recalled, "He said this would be the first holidays he would be spending without her."[3] Frey believed Scott's wife had died and thanked Peterson for sharing the painful story. When she asked Scott if he was ready to have a serious relationship with her, Scott said yes. On the same day Scott told Frey about his late wife, he bought a secondhand boat.

Frey had no idea that Scott was keeping secrets from her. Though he pretended to be single and childless, he had been married for five years, and his wife was heavily pregnant with their first child. Unbeknownst to her, Frey was not Scott's first affair partner.

On December 14, Scott told Laci he had to go on a business trip, so she attended a Christmas party alone. However, that night, Scott brought Frey roses and took her to a formal Christmas party. He spent the night at Frey's house, and the next day he told her he was going on a trip to Maine with his parents for the holidays. Scott said he was traveling to Europe after Christmas for business and to celebrate New Year's Eve. Both stories were lies, as Scott planned to go home to Laci in Modesto.

Frey didn't suspect anything was wrong until she asked Scott where she should send his Christmas gift. He gave her information for a post office box in Modesto. This didn't make sense to

SUSPICIOUS SEARCHES

After Laci Peterson disappeared, investigators scoured the couple's internet history for clues. They found that on December 7, 2002, Scott looked at online ads for used boats. The next day, he searched for information about ocean currents in San Francisco Bay.

Frey because Modesto was 80 miles (129 km) from Sacramento, where Scott had told her he lived. "That was really the first time that my heart sunk," said Frey. "I got teary-eyed. It was just really the first time that I felt things weren't sounding right."[4]

Over the next few days, Scott called Frey several times. Each time, he lied about where he was. On December 23, Scott said he was in Maine with his father, going duck hunting. In fact, he was home in Modesto.

Frey did not hear from Scott on December 24 or 25. On December 26, when Scott was supposed to be on a flight to Paris, France, Frey called his cell phone to leave a message. She was startled when Scott answered. He tried to explain that he was still in New York. But at this point, Frey was suspicious. She asked if Scott had another girlfriend or wife, but he assured her he did not.

Frey was unconvinced and uneasy. Scott's stories were not lining up. Then a friend showed her a newspaper article about a missing pregnant woman from Modesto. The woman was Laci Peterson, and the article mentioned her husband, Scott, and his occupation. Frey realized that her boyfriend was the missing woman's husband.

"I was in shock," Frey says. "I was crying, I have no idea how long. I was just trembling, and I was like, 'It is him.'"[5] As Scott's lies unraveled, Frey picked up the phone and dialed the number for the Modesto Police Department hotline.

Detective Allen Brocchini joined the Stanislaus County CAP Unit in 2000.

Call to Police

On December 30, Amber Frey called the Modesto Police Department and spoke to Detective Brocchini. She told Brocchini about her relationship with Scott and how he had insisted that he was single. Brocchini asked Frey if she would help the police by staying in contact with Scott without telling him she had talked to the police. Frey agreed. Brocchini raced to find Grogan and Buehler and called an emergency meeting. This could be the break they needed in the case.

On December 31, Scott called Frey to wish her a happy New Year. He claimed he was in Paris, though Frey knew he was still in California. Scott didn't know she'd caught on. He also did

Scott called Frey during Laci's vigil. He told her the background noise was from the crowd at the Eiffel Tower.

not know that Frey had talked to the police about him just a day earlier.

A Candlelight Vigil

Though Scott had told Frey he was in Paris, he actually spent New Year's Eve at a candlelight vigil for Laci. More than 1,000 people gathered at East La Loma Park for the vigil, with dozens of Laci's friends, classmates, and former teachers filling the park. Many of the gathered people held glowing candles. News trucks lined the streets to report on the event. Laci's and Scott's parents and siblings stood on a makeshift stage and took turns speaking to the crowd. They urged the community not to give up and to keep looking for Laci.

Many thought it was strange that although Scott was present at the vigil, he did not join his and Laci's families on the stage. He did not speak to reporters and avoided television cameras. As with previous media appearances, Scott stayed away from the spotlight.

Recorded Conversations

Detectives asked Frey to record her phone calls with Scott and gave her a recording device. For days, Scott continued to call and pretend to be in Europe while still in California. Eventually, Frey recorded more than 300 phone calls with him.[6]

In one of their recorded conversations on January 6, 2003, Scott finally confessed to Frey that he had lied. He told her he was married, and his wife had disappeared before Christmas. And he admitted that he had been in Modesto with their

Frey recorded more than 12 hours of phone calls with Scott.

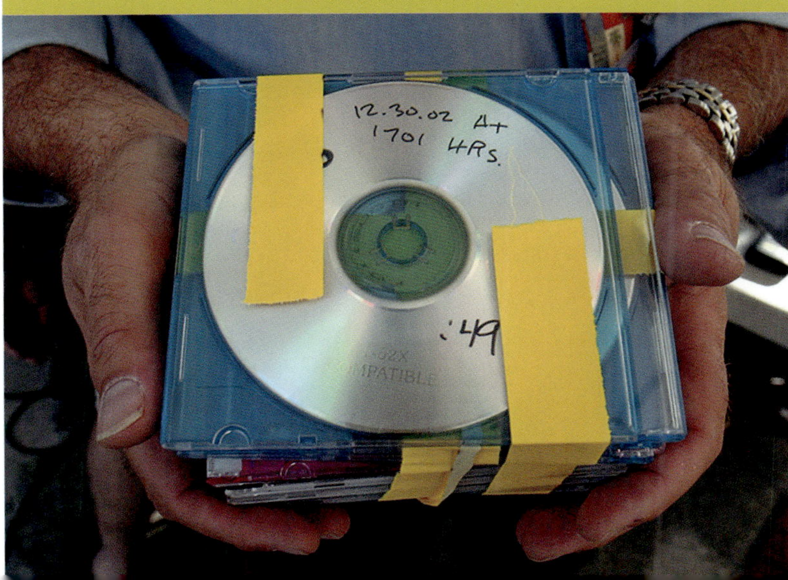

families searching for Laci. Frey questioned him about his marriage and unborn child. Scott repeated that he could not answer her questions because the media were hunting him, and he wanted to protect Frey from the chaos. When Frey asked if she should be afraid of him, Scott replied, "I am not an evil person. . . . I would never hurt anyone."[7]

Even after admitting the truth about his marriage, Scott lied to Frey. He told her he had taken a polygraph test, which he did not. And he told her that the police, his family, and his attorney had advised him not to go in front of the public, which was another lie.

Betrayed

Meanwhile, Laci's and Scott's families remained unaware of Scott's affair with Frey. They felt strongly that he was not involved in her disappearance. On live television with journalist Larry King, Sharon Rocha said she stood firmly behind Scott. Lee Peterson said that Laci's disappearance had devastated his son. "I've never seen him so sad," Scott's father said during the interview. "He's just what you'd expect from someone who is missing their wife and baby." Amy Rocha, Laci's half sister, spoke in support of Scott as well. "We have no question in our mind about Scott. He's part of our family."[8]

On January 15, 2003, detectives decided to tell Scott's and Laci's families about Scott's affair. The police knew that a tabloid newspaper, the *National Enquirer*, was about to run an explosive story that linked Scott to an unnamed woman. Police knew that woman was Amber Frey. Detectives wanted the family to know the truth before they read it in the paper.

About two weeks after Laci went missing, Scott called his satellite television service and added explicit adult channels to their subscription, something many found suspicious if he believed his wife was coming home.

The Modesto police set up a private meeting with Sharon Rocha and Ron Grantski. They told the couple about Scott's affair and the impending newspaper story. Sharon and Ron were stunned. As the detectives detailed Scott and Frey's relationship, Sharon broke down in tears. Laci's parents, who had been steadfast in their support of Scott, suddenly suspected him of the worst.

"Why did he have to kill her?" Sharon asked.[9] Later, Sharon would admit that she had doubts about Scott before learning about his affair, and the news about Frey confirmed her suspicions. "I mean, I knew," she said in a 2006 interview. "When they said those words, I knew any of the suspicions I'd been having, you know, all of his unusual behavior, his odd behavior, I knew that moment. That just confirmed everything I was afraid to admit to myself and afraid to even think about. That he had killed her."[10]

Frey hired attorney Gloria Allred to help navigate the fallout from Scott's affair.

On January 16, the *National Enquirer* story broke. Although the article did not identify Frey by name, it included pictures of Frey and Scott. The news set reporters in a frenzy, and they began to search for the mystery woman's identity.

Speaking to the Press

On January 24, reporters found Scott's mystery woman. Reporters and photographers surrounded the building where Frey worked and attempted to contact her. Frey suggested that she make a public statement to appease the press so they would leave her alone, and Buehler agreed that it was a good idea. They prepared for a press conference later that evening. At the press conference, Frey admitted to a brief romantic relationship with Scott but emphasized that he had told her he was unmarried. She told the public that she sympathized with Laci's family and prayed that Laci would be found safe.

The shocking revelation that Scott had been having an affair quickly turned Laci's family and public opinion against him. They began to question whether he was hiding other information from them, such as information about what had happened to Laci.

Now that his affair was plastered across the national news, Scott suddenly became interested in doing interviews. He agreed to an interview with Diane Sawyer on *Good Morning America*. In the interview, Scott denied murdering his wife or having anything to do with her disappearance.

"Violence toward women is unapproachable," Scott said. "It is the most disgusting act to me." However, he publicly admitted to the affair with Frey. He acknowledged it was inappropriate and insisted that he had told

MERINGUE MISHAP

The morning that Laci was reported missing, Scott told investigators she was watching a cooking show that talked about meringues. At first, Scott said he left his home at 9:30 a.m. Yet the meringue segment did not air until 9:48 a.m., which proved Scott was home later than he had originally claimed. Since a neighbor found the Petersons' dog wandering at 10:18 a.m., this new evidence made the theory of Laci being attacked while walking her dog seem unlikely. There was a very small window of time in which the attack could have occurred.

police about the affair as soon as his wife went missing. Scott also claimed that Laci knew about the affair. He said he had told her about it in early December and that though she was unhappy, they were dealing with it. "It wasn't anything that would break us apart," he said.[11]

Reclassified as Homicide

Since December 24, 2002, police had treated Laci Peterson's disappearance as a missing person case. On March 4, 2003, the Modesto Police Department announced that the case had been reclassified as a homicide. Although the police department did not explain what prompted the reclassification, Detective Grogan issued a statement. "As the investigation has progressed," Grogan said, "we have increasingly come to believe that Laci Peterson is the victim of a violent crime."[12]

Scott told the media that he was glad that Frey revealed the affair.

Police had a suspect in their sights: Scott Peterson. They were convinced that Scott had killed Laci so that he could pursue a romance with Frey. Scott had been leading a double life, acting as a doting husband and excited father-to-be while driving at least once a week to be with Frey. Detectives believed he had finally grown tired of the charade and decided to get rid of his wife.

Though Scott said he immediately told investigators about Frey, police said he denied having an affair multiple times during the investigation.

CHAPTER FIVE

DISCOVERY AND ARREST

On April 13, 2003, Michael Looby and Nicole Belanger were walking their dog near the Richmond Inner Harbor on the northern shore of San Francisco Bay when their dog stopped in a grassy area and began sniffing at something intently. Looby walked over to see what had captured the dog's interest and stared in horror. It was a baby's body.

Bodies Found

Looby and Belanger asked a nearby resident to call the police. When the Richmond police and fire departments arrived, they discovered a fetus lying among leaves and other debris. The body was in bad shape, and investigators could not determine the baby's sex or race. After photographing the scene, investigators gently wrapped the body in a towel and sent it to the Contra Costa coroner's office.

A makeshift memorial was created on the edge of San Francisco Bay after two bodies washed ashore.

A preliminary police report ruled the infant's death as unexplained. Investigators estimated the infant was only a few days old, but they were not able to determine a cause of death. A notification about the discovery was sent to law enforcement agencies throughout California. The following day, Detective Grogan learned about the dead infant right before he went into court to testify in another case. During his lunch break, he got a phone call. Another body had been found.

Park visitors at East Bay Regional Park reported finding a body shortly before noon on April 14. The body was that of an adult woman and had washed ashore east of Brooks Island, close to where Scott said he had been fishing on Christmas Eve. The woman's body was wearing a bra and the remnants of pants, and her head, forearms, and lower legs were missing.

Grogan spoke with Lieutenant Pete Small of the East Bay Regional Park Police. He instructed the officer to photograph, videotape, and recover the body and evidence as soon as possible. He also asked that no details about the crime scene or condition of the body be released to the press.

Although it was impossible to know at this point if the deceased woman was Laci Peterson, some evidence suggested it might be. The woman wore a nursing bra, sometimes preferred by pregnant women, and wore pants with a maternity label. Also, the fact that the body of an infant had been recovered nearby the day before and both bodies had been in

The two bodies were found within approximately three miles (5 km) of Berkeley Marina.[1]

the water for some time led many to suspect that Laci and her child had finally been found.

Autopsy

At the Contra Costa coroner's office, the autopsy on the recovered infant, which they called Baby Doe, had begun. Coroner Brian Peterson (unrelated to Scott) performed the autopsy. Peterson determined that Baby Doe was a full-term male infant that had been dead for some time. He estimated the fetus's gestational age to be between 33 and 38 weeks.[2]

Because the infant's body condition was poor, Peterson could not tell if the fetus had been born alive or if the infant had died in the womb. Some evidence indicated the baby most likely had not been born alive. Peterson was also unable to say if the baby had taken a breath. He was unable to determine the infant's cause of death.

Next, the coroner's office performed an autopsy on the woman's body, labeled as Jane Doe. The condition of Jane

PROTECTED BY HIS MOTHER

Forensic scientists noted that the remains of Laci's son were in relatively good condition compared with her remains. The scientists said the fetus's body appeared to have been protected from the water and elements for a length of time. They concluded that the unborn child was protected in Laci's womb for several weeks after their deaths until the infant was eventually separated from her body in the bay.

Doe's body suggested the victim had been in the water for a long time. The body had significant decomposition and was missing the head, forearms, and lower legs. Because there was no evidence of tool marks at the bone joints of the missing limbs, the coroner concluded the victim had been weighted, and a combination of the water's currents and the body's decomposition had caused the limbs to pull apart. In addition, the coroner found that the victim had sustained several broken ribs shortly before death. However, the autopsy could not determine a definite cause of death.

Because of the condition of the bodies, investigators could not immediately confirm if the remains belonged to Laci and her son. Only DNA tests would be able to identify the deceased. Fortunately, forensic scientists could extract usable DNA samples from the bone and tissue of both victims. They compared the samples to samples from Laci's mother and father and from Scott.

Tracking Scott Peterson

As investigators combed the shoreline for any additional evidence, Detective Brocchini searched for Scott. He knew Scott was in the San Diego area because detectives had placed a GPS tracker on his car. The city was close to the Mexican border, and detectives feared Scott would try to flee the country now that Laci's body had potentially been found.

FAREWELL SERVICE

On May 5, 2003, thousands of people packed the First Baptist Church in Modesto for a farewell service for Laci Peterson on what would have been her twenty-eighth birthday. Because the young mother-to-be's story had touched so many people across the country, the service was televised nationally. Laci's family and friends gave a series of eulogies and remembered the young woman who had made an impression on so many.

However, the detectives learned that Scott was no longer driving his white 2002 Dodge Dakota truck, possibly because he suspected he was being tracked. Agents watched his parents' house, his father's business, and other locations but could not immediately locate Scott.

On April 16, Brocchini learned through wiretaps on Scott's cell phone that he was checking his voice mail from a relative's home in San Diego. The relative had permitted Scott to stay at the house and use their car. Brocchini sent surveillance units to the area.

Agents reported seeing Scott walking around the neighborhood. They noted, however, that his appearance had significantly changed since the last time they had seen him. Scott was no longer clean-shaven and had grown a thick goatee. He had also bleached his dark hair, eyebrows, and beard an orange-blond shade. With Scott located, the agents secured an arrest warrant and waited.

Arrest

Detectives monitored Scott's movements for days, waiting for positive identification of the recovered remains before arresting him. However, detectives feared Scott would try to escape to Mexico if they waited much longer. On April 18, they decided to move in and make the arrest.

Police arrested Scott in La Jolla, California, near the Torrey Pines Golf Club. He did not resist as officers handcuffed him. He merely asked if the agents had found his wife and son.

At the time of his arrest, Scott was driving a Mercedes-Benz erratically. A search of his car revealed nearly $15,000 in cash, three credit cards, his brother's driver's license, backpacking

Investigators suspected that Scott may have changed his appearance to avoid capture.

and camping supplies, clothing, four cell phones, Mexican currency, a gun, and more.[3] It was evident that Scott had packed to go somewhere for a long time.

Later that day, the DNA results came in. Jane Doe was positively identified as Laci Peterson, and Baby Doe was Scott and Laci's child. By midnight, detectives had driven Scott back to Modesto, where he was booked and charged with two counts of first-degree murder. In a press conference at police headquarters, Police Chief Roy Wasden expressed sympathy for Laci's family, calling the death a tragedy. "We've really tried for, hoped for, prayed for a different outcome than the one that has occurred," Wasden said. "While it's happy to have a conclusion, it's truly sad to have that conclusion."[4]

While police declined to comment on the case details, California attorney general Bill Lockyer said the case against Scott was solid. "This is a compellingly strong case," he said. "I would call the odds slam-dunk that he is going to be convicted."[5]

DEFENSE ATTORNEY MARK GERAGOS

After Scott was arrested and charged with Laci's and Conner's murders, his family hired celebrity defense lawyer Mark Geragos from Los Angeles. Geragos had represented high-profile clients previously, including actress Winona Ryder and pop superstar Michael Jackson. Geragos replaced the two public defenders initially assigned to the case.

Charged with Murder

On April 21, Scott appeared in the Stanislaus County Superior Court for his arraignment. The judge read Scott's charges, announcing that Scott was charged with two counts of first-degree murder, one for the death of his wife, Laci, and a second for Conner. Scott pleaded not guilty to all charges. Under California law, because Laci was pregnant at the time of the alleged murder, the charges against Scott carried a special enhancement. This meant he was not eligible for bail. If found guilty, Scott could be sentenced to death. Scott was also assigned a public defender. Later, well-known defense attorney Mark Geragos would take his case.

After the arraignment, the Rocha family and friends appeared at an emotional press conference. Sharon Rocha praised the Modesto police and the work they had done. "Laci and her unborn child did not deserve to die. They certainly did not deserve to be dumped in the bay and sent to a watery grave," said Rocha. She also referred to her son-in-law without using his name. She said, "I can only hope that the sound of Laci's voice begging for her life, begging for the life of her unborn child, is heard over and over again in the mind of that person every day for the rest of his life."[6]

After his arrest, Scott Peterson was held in solitary confinement for his own safety at the Stanislaus County Men's Jail.

CHAPTER SIX

THE TRIAL OF SCOTT PETERSON

On June 1, 2004, the trial of Scott Peterson for the murder of his wife and their unborn child began. Several months earlier, in January 2004, a judge granted the defense's request to move the trial out of Stanislaus County, where Laci was from. The trial was moved nearly two hours away to San Mateo County.

As the trial opened at the San Mateo County Superior Court, a jury of six women and six men listened to the arguments and evidence presented by both sides. Presiding over the trial was Judge Alfred Delucchi, a judge who had come out of retirement to hear the case. The families of Laci and Scott sat on opposite sides of the courtroom while journalists and observers filled the middle and back rows of the room. All participants were prepared for a long trial; the case was expected to last for four to five months.

During the trial, detectives testified that one of Scott's friends recalled him talking about the best way to dispose of a body. The method he described was nearly identical to what police believe happened to Laci.

NO CAMERAS

In February 2003, Judge Alfred Delucchi banned cameras throughout the Scott Peterson trial. Attorneys for news channels had argued that the public had a right to see the proceedings, but the judge disagreed. Both the prosecution and the defense supported the ban on cameras and said such distractions would contribute to a circus-like atmosphere around the trial.

Opening Statements

Deputy District Attorneys Rick Distaso and Dave Harris led the prosecution's case. In his opening statement, which lasted four hours, Distaso outlined a case built on piece after piece of circumstantial evidence. Distaso focused on Scott's changing alibi and his affair with Amber Frey as his alleged motive. He highlighted the suspicious details of Scott's movements when Laci disappeared. He told jurors that Scott had lied about when he left his home, and that cell phone records would prove it.

Even though there was no murder weapon or physical evidence directly tying Scott to Laci's and Conner's deaths, Distaso argued that the overwhelming circumstantial evidence was enough to prove Peterson's guilt beyond a reasonable doubt. The prosecution claimed that Scott's lies and inconsistencies were meant to cover up his guilt in the murder of his wife and child. "Ladies and gentlemen," Distaso proclaimed at the trial, "this is a commonsense case. At the end of this case, I'm going to ask you to find the defendant guilty of the murder of Laci Peterson as well as the murder of his son, Conner."[1]

The next day, defense attorney Mark Geragos made his opening statement. He insisted Scott was innocent. Geragos told the jury that although his client had cheated on his wife, it did not mean he had murdered her. He emphasized that Scott loved Laci and was eager to become a dad, and there was no reason for him to throw it all away because of his brief involvement with Amber Frey. "You want to say his behavior is boorish, we are not going to dispute that," Geragos said. "But the fact is that this is a murder case, and there has to be evidence in a murder case."[2]

The defense attorney emphasized that the prosecution had no forensic evidence linking Scott to the murders. In addition, Geragos promised the defense would present medical experts and eyewitnesses to support the defense's theory that Laci had been kidnapped while Scott was miles away fishing in San Francisco Bay.

Scott's attorneys said that several unrelated witnesses reported seeing Laci within a one-mile (1.6 km) radius of the Peterson home on December 24.[3]

The Prosecution's Case

Over the next four months, the prosecution presented its case against Scott to the jury. It called 174 witnesses to testify

Billboards outside the courthouse urged passersby to say whether they thought Scott was innocent or guilty.

over 19 weeks, including the Petersons' housekeeper, family, and friends, and the police officers who had investigated the case. Each time, defense attorney Mark Geragos skillfully cross-examined the witnesses, using them to bolster his defense case and highlight the weaknesses of the prosecution's case. For example, during Geragos's cross-examination of Amy Rocha, Laci's sister, the attorney was able to get Rocha to admit on the stand that she had previously insisted Scott was the last person who would hurt anyone.

The prosecution plodded at a slow and steady pace with its case. Some court observers worried that the jury was becoming overwhelmed by the many witnesses and pieces of information. "It does seem like the prosecution has maybe put the jury to sleep," said California defense attorney Steve Cron

during the trial. "They put on so much evidence, much of it of marginal relevance to the case, that I think strategically, they didn't handle it well. They anticipated what the defense would be in some areas and attempted to rebut it before the defense presented it to jurors. The textbook way of doing it is you put on your case, the defense puts on their case, and then if there's something you like to challenge you do it on rebuttal."[4]

Frey Takes the Stand

The prosecution's star witness was Amber Frey. When she took the stand in August 2004, many legal observers worried the prosecution's case was in trouble. There was very little direct physical evidence against Scott, so the prosecution's case was almost entirely based on pieces of circumstantial evidence.

FIRST JUROR REMOVED

In June 2003, the judge removed Justin Falconer from the 12-person jury and replaced him with an alternate juror. Falconer admitted to talking about media coverage of the trial with his girlfriend, which was against jury rules. After being dismissed, he told reporters that he would have found Scott innocent if he had remained on the jury.

However, Frey's testimony allowed prosecutors to tie the pieces together and paint a picture of Scott's guilt. Her testimony lasted seven days and included many recorded conversations with Scott. She showed Scott was a liar, a cheater, and a man who would romance his girlfriend while his pregnant wife was missing.

On the stand, Frey came across as credible and honest. Her careful questioning of Scott in the recorded conversations proved incredibly impactful on the jury. In one example, the jury listened intently as the prosecution played a taped conversation from January 6, 2003, only 11 days after Laci had gone missing. On the tape, Frey asks Scott what Laci's response was when he told her about their affair.

"Fine," Scott said on the recording.

"Fine?" asked Frey, disbelief in her voice. "An eight-month [pregnant] woman fine about another woman?" The jury laughed.[5]

Another conversation from January 6 also appeared to impact the jury. In the recording, Scott reads Frey a romantic poem, which includes the line "my hands around your waist." When Frey said that she did not understand the line, Scott explained, "You know, my hands around your waist, like, you know, anchors for people."[6] His explanation was uncomfortably similar to the prosecution's allegation that he had attached concrete anchors to Laci's body and dumped her into San Francisco Bay.

"That is as close to a smoking gun as we're going to get," said Bay Area defense attorney Daniel Horowitz, who was observing the trial. "How the heck does he get the words 'anchors' and a human being in the same sentence if he doesn't know how Laci died?"[7]

On the stand, Frey was a strong witness. She avoided eye contact with Scott and the jurors and answered questions in a soft voice. She showed little emotion during most of her testimony. When cross-examined by Geragos, Frey admitted that Scott had never said he loved her but remained firm in her testimony. Legal expert Michael Cardoza analyzed Frey's testimony, saying, "She appears humble, as someone who has done the right thing, and didn't do it for money."[8]

The Defense's Case

Throughout the prosecution's case, Peterson's lead defense attorney, Mark Geragos, cross-examined prosecution witnesses, poked holes in their testimonies, and tried to raise doubt in the minds of the jury. For example, a prosecution expert witness admitted under cross-examination that investigators had found no blood or physical evidence on Scott's boat or in his home that linked him to Laci's murder. Also, Geragos was able to suggest through cross-examination of several witnesses that the police had neglected to investigate other leads in the Laci Peterson case thoroughly and had focused solely on her husband.

"Prosecutors had offered a motive, that he [Peterson] was tired of this marriage, that she [Laci] became this obstacle to his continuing an affair with Amber Frey," said James Cohen, associate professor of law and director of clinical education at New York's Fordham University. "But prosecutors left their witnesses open to be used by Geragos to his advantage repeatedly, revealing loose ends in their case and having them stumble over certain points. After a while, repeated stumbles begin to make the defense's case look more credible in the jury's eyes."[9]

WHAT HAPPENED TO AMBER FREY?

After the trial, Amber Frey published a memoir titled *Witness for the Prosecution of Scott Peterson*. She told reporters that while her involvement with Scott was a story for many observers, it was a very real and painful part of her life. Since then, she has done her best to put that part of her life behind her. She is now the mother of two children and continues to work as a massage therapist.

When it was the defense's turn, Geragos called 14 witnesses over six days of testimony, much less time than the prosecution had spent. Defense witnesses included Scott's parents, Lee and Jackie Peterson. They worked to explain his behavior, which some had interpreted as a sign of guilt. Jackie testified to explain why Scott had nearly $15,000 in cash on him when he was arrested. She said she had mistakenly withdrawn $10,000 of the money from Scott's bank account, which also had her name on it, to lend to his brother.[10] She said the money was in Scott's possession because she had returned it to Scott the day before his arrest. The defense also questioned Modesto police officer Michael Hicks about a robbery at a neighbor's home around the time Laci vanished and whether the robbery suspects may have been involved in Laci's murder.

The only time Scott cried during the trial was when his friend testified in his favor.

Another defense witness was gynecologist Dr. Charles March. The defense asked Dr. March to examine Laci's medical records and the prosecution witnesses' findings about the estimated date of her son Conner's death. March testified that based on bone measurements of the fetus and Laci's ultrasounds, he estimated that the date of Conner's death was most likely December 29, 2002, at the earliest, five days after Laci disappeared. March's testimony contradicted the

When Conner's body was found, a piece of tape was looped around his neck. The defense and prosecution argued about whether this could have happened in the bay or if it was placed by the murderer. If it was placed by the murderer, Conner was born alive.

prosecution's claim that Scott had murdered Laci on or around December 24.

However, under cross-examination from prosecutors, March admitted that he had based his findings on the assumption that Laci had first learned of her pregnancy on June 9, when she told a friend she was expecting. He admitted that there was nothing in Laci's medical records to show she had first learned of her pregnancy on June 9. She could have known earlier, which could impact the estimated date of Conner's death.

The defense did not call Scott Peterson to the stand. Despite the defense's air of certainty, many legal experts felt the defense's case had some holes. "None of the promises made by (defense lawyer) Mark Geragos during opening statements have been fulfilled," said former prosecutor Dean Johnson at the time. "He promised to show the baby was born alive and there's been no evidence of that. He promised to show that Peterson was stone-cold innocent, and he hasn't done that, so this is now a case that's going to come down to reasonable doubt."[11]

Closing Arguments

After the defense concluded its case, the prosecution and defense delivered closing arguments to the jury. For the prosecution, Distaso showed the jury an aerial photograph of San Francisco Bay and pointed to the rocky beach where the remains of Laci and Conner were discovered. He also indicated the area only a few miles away where Scott alleged he was fishing on the day Laci vanished. He outlined Scott's motive for murder, saying that Scott was tired of his dull, married life and did not want to become a father. He explained that Scott decided that killing Laci was his way out.

Distaso walked the jury through what the prosecution alleged happened to Laci. He accused Scott of strangling or smothering his wife on the night of December 23 or the morning of December 24. The prosecutor told the jury that Scott wrapped Laci's body in a blue tarp, placed it in his truck, and drove it to his warehouse. Then, he transferred the body to his boat, sailed out into San Francisco Bay, weighted Laci's body with homemade cement anchors, and dumped her into the bay. He asserted that Scott Peterson was the only one "we know without any doubt that was in the exact location in the exact spot where Laci and Conner washed ashore. . . . That alone is proof beyond a reasonable doubt in this case. You can take that fact to the bank and you can convict this man of murder," Distaso said.[12]

When it was the defense's turn, Geragos pointed out that everyone supported Scott until they learned of his affair. He emphasized that while Scott may have been unfaithful to his wife, it did not mean he was a murderer. Geragos told the jury that the police had decided Scott was guilty early in the case and neglected to investigate other leads that pointed away from him. He pointed out flaws in the prosecution's case and noted that police had not found a murder weapon, physical evidence, or witnesses that tied Scott to the murder. He urged the jury to find that the prosecution had not proven their case beyond a reasonable doubt.

The Jury Decides

After two days of closing arguments, jury deliberations began on the afternoon of November 3, 2004, with the 12-person jury sequestered in a hotel. The jury would remain there until it determined whether Scott killed his wife, and if so, whether he should be convicted of first-degree murder or second-degree murder. During their deliberations, the jurors could review and consider all trial evidence. That included testimony from more

In Rick Distaso's closing statement, he pointed out that the fishing lures Scott claimed to have used were still sealed in their packaging.

than 185 witnesses, hours of audio recordings, and numerous documents. It also included physical evidence, such as part of a blue tarp and a handmade cement anchor.[13]

Approximately 32 hours into deliberations, the judge announced that Juror #7 was replaced with an alternate juror. Some legal experts speculated that Juror #7 had gone online to research something about the case, which was prohibited. The juror's replacement meant the entire jury would have to restart its deliberations.

The following day, the judge announced that another juror was being replaced. This time Juror #5, who had been elected the spokesperson of the jury, had asked the judge to be released from the case. An alternate juror replaced him, and the jury once again restarted its deliberations.

CHAPTER SEVEN

GUILTY OF MURDER

On November 12, 2004, the jury in the Scott Peterson trial notified the court that they had reached a verdict. Scott Peterson smiled and talked with one of his defense lawyers as he waited for the jury to return to the courtroom. Nearby, in the standing-room-only courtroom, the family and friends of Laci waited somberly for the jury's decision.

After the 12 jurors returned to the courtroom, the court clerk read the verdict. "We the jury in the above-entitled cause find the defendant Scott Lee Peterson guilty of the crime of the murder of Laci Denise Peterson," the clerk read.[1] As the word *guilty* was read, Laci's mother, Sharon Rocha, began to sob and collapsed into the arms of her son while several of Laci's childhood friends gasped and burst into tears. On the other side of the room, Scott's mother, Jackie Peterson, slightly

Scott said he was shocked by the jury's verdict.

EXTRA
GUILTY
Crowds cheer verdict
tomorrow's Daily News
FREE

bowed her head. Scott's father, Lee Peterson, was not in the courtroom.

As he listened to the verdict, Scott Peterson showed no emotion. He kept his chin up and glanced between the judge and jury as the clerk finished reading. Later, in a 2021 interview with ABC, Scott described his feelings as he heard the guilty verdict. "It was crazy," Scott said. "It was like this amazing, horrible physical reaction that I had. Everything just went kind of silent or I couldn't hear anything. . . . I couldn't feel anything. I couldn't feel my feet on the floor. I couldn't feel the chair I was sitting in."[2]

The jury convicted Scott of first-degree murder for the death of Laci and convicted him of second-degree murder for the death of Conner. The judge asked each of the 12 jurors to confirm the guilty verdict. One by one, each juror replied, "Yes."[3] As the jurors left the courtroom, one turned to Sharon Rocha and nodded.

Crowds Cheer Verdict

Hundreds of people gathered outside the San Mateo County courthouse to listen to a live audio feed from the courtroom. As the guilty verdict was announced, cheers erupted from the crowd. Camera crews from numerous national, cable, and local networks captured reactions around the courthouse. Local newspapers printed special editions with headlines that read

"Guilty" and "Crowds Cheer Verdict."[4] In Laci's hometown of Modesto, drivers honked their horns and restaurant customers cheered as news of the guilty verdict spread.

As they left the courthouse, Laci's parents did not speak to the press, but Sharon Rocha smiled, and Ron Grantski gave the crowd a thumbs-up signal. One of Laci's relatives, Harvey Kemple, who testified during the trial, said the family was pleased with the verdict. Sharon Rocha's cousin, Gwen Kemple, said it was a great day. Jackie Peterson received a different response from the crowd when she emerged from the courthouse after the verdict. As she walked slowly to her car, a woman shouted to ask if Jackie was still proud of her son.

Prosecutors also looked pleased as they left the courtroom. However, Stanislaus County district attorney James Brazelton noted that their work was not yet done. The trial's penalty phase to determine Scott's sentence still had to be held. Jurors would be given a short break before returning to the courtroom to listen as the attorneys for both sides presented witnesses and arguments as to whether Scott should be sentenced to life in prison or receive the death penalty. Family members of both Scott and Laci were expected to take the stand.

Legal experts were split on what sentence the jury would return.

Scott was ordered to pay $10,000 in restitution for Laci's funeral expenses.[5]

The final jury deliberations took only seven hours.

Some believed jurors would be unlikely to vote for the death penalty in a case that relied heavily on circumstantial evidence, as the judge had told the jury that doubts were allowed to influence their votes. Yet others thought the jury was prepared to sentence Scott to death. "The speed that they came in [with a verdict] is an indication that they are not feeling sympathetic," said University of San Francisco law professor Robert Talbot. "They are feeling strong against him."[6]

The Trial's Penalty Phase

The penalty phase of Scott's trial began on November 30, 2004. The defense had unsuccessfully asked the court for a new jury in Los Angeles, claiming Peterson could not get fair sentencing in San Mateo County because of the public feeling against him. However, the court denied this request, and the existing jury remained in place to decide Scott's sentence.

The prosecution asked the jury to sentence Scott to death for his crimes. Several of Laci's family members and friends took the stand to give victim impact statements. They spoke about who Laci was and what she meant to them. They explained to the jury the pain and loss that her death and the death of her child had caused them.

Laci's mother, Sharon Rocha, was the final prosecution witness. Sharon's testimony was the most emotional for many people in the courtroom. She told the jury about the wonderful daughter Scott had taken away from her.

"Laci was just somebody that people gravitated to," Sharon said. "She had a personality that made people feel comfortable. She was an upbeat person. She was more of a leader than a follower. She was involved. She followed her heart. She would fight for her beliefs, and when she wanted something, she went after it."[7] As the prosecution displayed a series of photos of a young Laci, Sharon described each to the jury.

JUROR REACTION

After the trial was over, a few of the jurors talked about their decision to convict Scott. Jury foreman Steve Cardosi was a firefighter and paramedic. He said that the accumulation of evidence presented by the prosecution convinced him. He also said the fact that Scott's alibi, fishing in San Francisco Bay, put him near where the remains of his wife and child were found made him certain of Scott's guilt.

During her testimony, Sharon broke down when describing how she had spent her first Mother's Day without Laci. She told the jury how she had spent most of that day on the floor, unable to bear the knowledge that Laci would never be a mother herself. She turned and shouted at Scott, "She wanted to be a mother! Divorce is always an option, not murder!"[8]

Throughout her testimony, Sharon's voice shook with grief and, at times, rage. She told the court about having nightmares about how Laci and Conner had died and her anguish over the condition of Laci's body. Sharon talked about her panic when Laci went missing and her desperation to bring her home safely. "I begged for whoever had her to bring her home, to let her go, tell us where she was. And there was somebody who knew all along and you wouldn't tell us! Instead, you just let us go through this every day!" she lashed out at Scott.[9]

Sharon Rocha's emotional testimony moved many in the courtroom. Several jurors wept openly as she spoke, while

Sharon Rocha, *left*, called Scott evil, self-centered, and a coward.

many of Laci's relatives sobbed. Even some journalists and legal experts who had covered the trial for months broke down in tears listening to the grieving mother.

Pleading for Scott's Life

The following day, jurors heard from the defense. Attorney Pat Harris argued that Scott did not deserve the death penalty and called many of Scott's family members and friends to testify on his behalf. Much of their testimony focused on Scott as a son, brother, child, and person who did not deserve to die, while offering few details about Scott's relationship with Laci.

LIFE INSURANCE

Scott had taken out a $250,000 life insurance policy on his wife, Laci.[10] After he was convicted of her murder, he was not eligible to collect the money due to a California law that prohibits criminals from profiting from their crimes. In 2005, a judge ruled that the money would go to Sharon Rocha.

Scott's father, Lee Peterson, took the stand first. He spoke about his love for his son and the sense of devastation he'd felt when he heard the guilty verdict. He talked about his son's work ethic and how he had never been a problem as a child or teen. When asked how he would feel if Scott were sentenced to death, Lee said, "Losing someone you loved and now having your son in this kind of jeopardy, it's not something I ever thought I'd have to go through. . . . I just can't imagine anything worse."[11]

When it was her turn on the stand, Jackie Peterson begged the jury to spare her son's life. She said that Laci had been like a daughter to her. She admitted that Scott was not perfect but said he had always been loving, kind, and gentle and insisted he was not the devil that the media portrayed. "If you were to take Scott away from us, it would be a whole family wiped off the face of the earth," Jackie told the jury. "It would be like Laci never existed."[12]

After a week of testimony, prosecutors and defense attorneys made their final statements. The prosecution called Scott "the worst kind of monster," while the defense asked the jury to reject more death.[13] After listening to both sides, Judge Alfred Delucchi instructed the jurors to decide between a sentence of death or life in prison without the possibility of parole.

Sentenced to Death Row

On December 14, 2004, the jury returned after three days of deliberations. They recommended that Scott be sentenced to death. After the decision was read, Scott remained emotionless, as he had for much of the trial. His family was also quiet.

On March 16, 2005, Judge Delucchi formally sentenced Scott to death for the murder of his pregnant wife. One by one,

WRONGFUL DEATH LAWSUIT

In 2007, Sharon Rocha filed two wrongful death civil lawsuits against Scott, one as an individual and a second as the executor of Laci's estate. Attorneys representing Rocha said that Laci's family wanted to ensure Scott faced the greatest amount of civil and criminal penalties possible under the legal system. In 2015, Rocha quietly dropped the lawsuits.

Laci Peterson's loved ones stood at a podium a few feet from Scott and addressed him. For many, it was an opportunity to let out their rage at the man who had killed their daughter, sister, and friend. Laci's brother, Brent Rocha, told Scott he had bought a gun to kill him but decided he would rather not give him an easy way out. Laci's father, Dennis Rocha, yelled, "You are going to burn in hell for this, you are. Your life is done." Sharon Rocha spoke on behalf of her unborn grandson and asked "Daddy" why he was killing "Mommy and me" and mourned the fact that Laci didn't have arms to hold her child or a head to kiss and smell him.[14]

At one point, the emotional addresses directed at Scott became too much for the Peterson family. Lee Peterson called Brent Rocha a liar and left the courtroom after the judge warned him to be quiet. Jackie Peterson soon followed her husband. When defense lawyers asked for the Petersons to be allowed to speak, the judge denied the request, saying it was not their daughter who had been murdered. The judge offered Scott the opportunity to make a statement. He declined.

CHAPTER EIGHT

YEARS OF APPEALS

A little after 3:00 a.m. on March 17, 2005, police drove Scott in a white, unmarked van from the county jail in Redwood City, San Mateo County, to San Quentin State Prison. Scott was secured with leg irons and shackles around his waist and wrists for the transport. At San Quentin, Scott would become the 644th prisoner to wait for execution at the prison.[1] The prison overlooked San Francisco Bay, not far from where the bodies of Laci and Conner had been recovered.

From 2005 to 2022, Scott lived behind bars at San Quentin. He and the other death row inmates were kept in a section away from the other inmates. Peterson lived in his cell and was allowed five hours a day outside in a shared yard to exercise or play chess. Death row inmates are permitted to shower three times a week. They can attend religious services and

In 2021, Scott was investigated as a suspect in the 1996 disappearance of Cal Poly student Kristin Smart. Another suspect was eventually convicted.

receive mail, phone calls, and visits from family and friends. The prisoners also have access to the prison's law library and may have a television, which they pay for, in their cells. According to prison officials, Peterson was a model prisoner with no rule violations since he had been in custody.

The Legal Battle Resumes

Although Scott's trial was over, more legal battles were beginning. In California, death row inmates have two ways to appeal their convictions. One way is to file a direct appeal, which argues that the court made errors during the trial. The second way to appeal is through filing a writ of habeas corpus. Through habeas corpus, defendants are allowed to plead their cases before a judge and generally introduce new evidence, findings, or information not considered during their original trials.

On July 6, 2012, Scott's new death penalty attorney, Cliff Gardner, filed a direct appeal of Scott's death sentence. In the appeal, Gardner argued the publicity surrounding Scott's

SAN QUENTIN STATE PRISON

San Quentin State Prison is the oldest correctional institution in California. Established in 1852, it was created as an answer to widespread crime in the state. Inmates worked to build the prison during the day and slept on a prison ship at night. Today, San Quentin is located 12 miles (19 km) north of the Golden Gate Bridge in San Francisco and houses California's death row prisoners.[2]

original trial had made it impossible for him to receive a fair trial. He argued that the trial should have been moved out of San Mateo County because of the intense publicity. "Before hearing even a single witness," Gardner argued, "nearly half of all prospective jurors admitted they had already decided Mr. Peterson was guilty of capital murder."[3]

***Habeas corpus* is Latin for "you shall have the body" and gives defendants the right to appear in court.**

In the appeal, Gardner also argued that mistakes made by Judge Delucchi, who died after the trial, prevented Peterson from receiving a fair trial. He claimed the judge automatically excluded potential jurors who said they were against the death penalty. Gardner argued those jurors should have been questioned more to determine if they could still decide the case fairly.

He also claimed that some of the prosecution's evidence should never have been shown to the jury. For example, he argued that evidence from a police dog that picked up Laci's scent at Berkeley Marina should have been excluded from the trial because the dog had a track record of being wrong more than half the time. In the 423-page appeal, Gardner listed numerous issues with the original trial that he believed negatively impacted his client, including errors, incorrect rulings, and juror misconduct.

Scott spent 17 years at San Quentin Prison.

For a death penalty case in California, the appeals process typically takes years to make its way through the courts. In addition, lawsuits in federal and state courts halted the practice of capital punishment in California. When Scott's appeal was filed in 2012, there were 725 inmates on death row in California, but no one had been executed in the state since 2006.[4]

In 2015, Scott Peterson's attorneys filed a second appeal. This appeal was a habeas corpus petition, which alleged that the criminal trial and its resulting conviction and sentencing violated Peterson's constitutional rights. Peterson's petition included many of the arguments from his 2012 appeal, with one notable addition. In the habeas corpus petition, Peterson's attorneys alleged that a replacement juror had lied about her background in a pretrial question and failed to disclose that she had been a victim of domestic violence while she was pregnant.

Death Sentence Overturned

In June 2020, more than 15 years after the murder of Laci Peterson, the California Supreme Court heard the appeal of Scott's death sentence. In the hearing, Scott's attorney Cliff Gardner asked the court to overturn his client's conviction and death sentence. He argued that Scott did not receive a fair trial because of the media attention, numerous judicial errors, and improper dismissal of potential jurors.

On August 24, 2020, the California Supreme Court announced its decision. The court ruled to uphold Scott's conviction in the murders of his wife and unborn child but agreed that the trial judge had made errors that impaired Scott's right to an impartial jury during sentencing. As such, they overturned his 2005 death sentence. "We reject Peterson's claim that he received an unfair trial as to guilt and thus affirm his convictions for murder," the court said. "But before the trial began, the trial court made a series of clear and significant errors in jury selection."[5]

MORATORIUM ON EXECUTIONS

In 2019, California governor Gavin Newsom announced a moratorium on executions in the state. Newsom used an executive order to grant reprieves to the 737 prisoners on California's death row at the time.[6] He also announced that he was closing down the state's execution chamber. Newsom said that he would not oversee any executions while he was the state's governor.

The court agreed with Scott's argument that potential jurors were improperly dismissed from the jury pool. "While a court may dismiss a prospective juror as unqualified to sit on a capital case if the juror's views on capital punishment would substantially impair his or her ability to follow the law," the justices said in a unanimous decision, "a juror may not be dismissed merely because he or she has expressed opposition to the death penalty as a general matter."[7]

Scott hung a picture of Laci on the wall of his cell in San Quentin Prison.

After the decision, the court noted that the prosecution could retry the penalty phase of Scott's trial. However, Stanislaus County district attorney Birgit Fladager announced that her office would not proceed with a retrial, and Peterson would be sentenced to life in prison without the possibility of parole. Fladager said that her office had spoken with Laci's family, and they had decided it would be too painful to live through the process of a trial again.

In October 2022, Scott was transferred from San Quentin's death row to Mule Creek State Prison in Ione, California. This facility is located in central California about an hour southeast of Sacramento. There, Scott was slated to serve his sentence of life without the possibility of parole.

Review of Juror Misconduct

In October 2020, the California Supreme Court ordered that Scott's case be sent back to the trial court in San Mateo County to consider whether the conviction should be overturned because of juror misconduct. The argument was part of Scott's habeas corpus petition, which outlined 19 claims for a new trial.

According to Scott's attorneys, Juror #7, Richelle Nice, lied on her pretrial jury questioning and falsely denied she had been a victim of a crime or involved in a lawsuit. When Nice was pregnant in 2000, she sought a restraining order against her boyfriend's ex-girlfriend, who she feared would harm her and her unborn child. "Someone who has gone through an experience where someone was threatening their unborn child will probably have a perspective on charges brought against a defendant for harming an unborn child," said Gardner. "They may come in with a bias that other people wouldn't have."[8]

After evidentiary hearings early in 2022, Judge Anne-Christine Massullo denied Scott's request for a new trial.

WHAT IS AN EVIDENTIARY HEARING?

An evidentiary hearing is a legal court proceeding in which eyewitnesses give testimony under oath and evidence is presented that is relevant to a case. The judge listens to the eyewitness testimony and evidence presented during the hearing. Then the judge decides which evidence can be used during the trial.

In her 55-page order, the judge concluded that while several of Nice's answers on the juror questionnaire were incorrect or incomplete, they "were not motivated by preexisting or improper bias against Petitioner, but instead were the result of combination of good faith misunderstanding of the questions and sloppiness in answering."[9]

Guilty or Innocent?

Although Judge Massullo denied Scott a new trial in 2022, his lawyers planned to file more appeals in the future. The process was expected to take years, if not decades, to complete. Meanwhile, throughout it all, Scott has steadfastly maintained his innocence. His lawyers and some family members argued that he has been wrongly convicted. Defense attorney Pat Harris addressed reporters in 2020, saying, "He's innocent—an innocent man's been sitting in jail for 15 years. It's time to get him out."[10]

Scott's sister-in-law, Janey Peterson, has become an outspoken advocate for his innocence. She has spoken to numerous news outlets about the case and has insisted that new evidence will show Scott did not commit the murders. "We will not stop fighting until Scott is free and we find who murdered Laci and Conner," she wrote in December 2022.[11] She insists that burglars kidnapped and murdered the young woman.

Yet many others believe Scott is rightfully behind bars for the murder of Laci and her unborn child. After Judge Massullo denied Scott a new trial in 2022, the Stanislaus County District Attorney's Office issued a statement expressing its hope the decision would bring Laci's family and friends peace. The statement read, "The family and friends of Laci have endured what only those who have lost someone to an act of senseless murder can ever begin to know. It has taken 20 years to reach this point and we hope that Judge Massullo's decision will finally bring them some measure of closure. Meanwhile, not a day has gone by that Laci's family and friends have not thought of her and Conner and missed them with all their hearts. We as a community share in their loss."[12]

Scott's appeal for a new trial was heard at San Mateo County Superior Court.

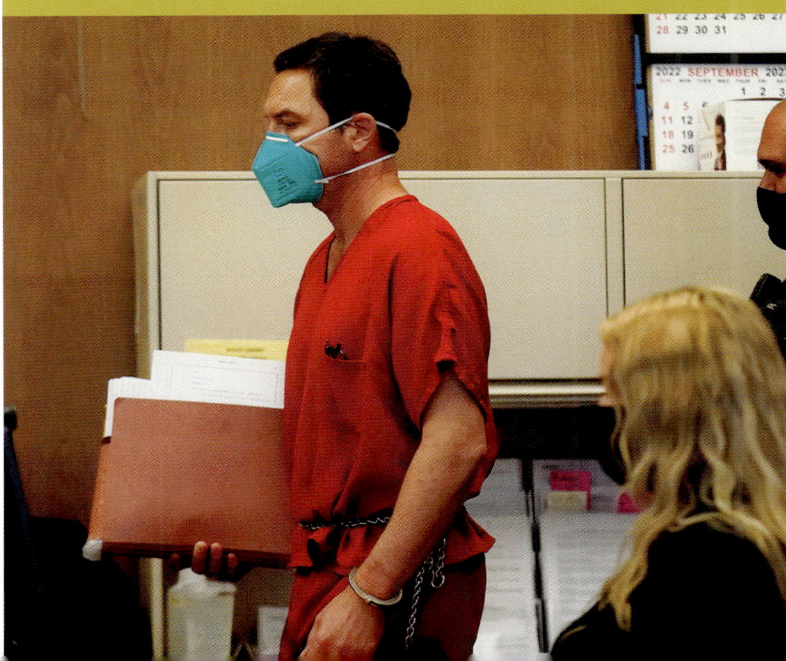

TIMELINE

1995

- Laci Rocha and Scott Peterson meet at a café and start dating.

1997

- Scott and Laci get married in an elegant ceremony at the Sycamore Mineral Springs Resort in San Luis Obispo, California.

2000

- Scott and Laci move to Modesto, California, and purchase a home together.

2002

- In November, Scott meets Amber Frey, a massage therapist, and begins an affair with her.
- In early December, Scott buys a used boat and researches San Francisco Bay current movements.
- On December 24, Laci's stepfather, Ron Grantski, calls the police to report Laci missing. Police conduct initial searches and interview Scott.
- On December 25, authorities launch a massive search to find Laci Peterson. Detectives investigate hundreds of leads, but there is no sign of the missing woman.
- On December 30, Frey calls the Modesto Police Department and tells them about her relationship with Scott. At the request of police, she begins recording her conversations with Scott.

2003

- On January 16, a *National Enquirer* story about Scott and a mystery woman hits newsstands.
- On January 24, Frey holds a press conference after reporters track her down at her workplace. She insists that she did not know Scott was married.
- On March 4, Modesto police reclassify the Laci Peterson case as a homicide.
- On April 13, the remains of a fetus are discovered near San Francisco Bay.
- On April 14, the remains of an adult woman are discovered near San Francisco Bay.

- On April 18, Scott is arrested near the Mexican border. He has dyed hair and is carrying $15,000 in cash and multiple credit cards and cell phones. Later that day, DNA testing confirms that the bodies found belong to Laci and their unborn son, Conner Peterson.
- On April 24, Scott is officially charged with the murders of Laci Peterson and their unborn child.

2004

- On November 12, the jury finds Scott guilty of the first-degree murder of Laci and the second-degree murder of Conner.
- On December 14, the jury recommends a sentence of death for Scott.

2005

- On March 16, the judge officially sentences Scott to death. Later that month, Scott enters San Quentin Prison.

2012

- In July, Scott files his first appeal.

2015

- Scott files a second appeal, a habeas corpus petition.

2020

- The California Supreme Court overturns Scott's death sentence. He is resentenced to life in prison without the possibility of parole. The court also orders that Scott's case be sent back to the trial court based on a claim of juror misconduct.

2022

- The court denies Scott's request for a new trial, but his lawyers plan to continue the appeal process.

ESSENTIAL FACTS

SIGNIFICANT EVENTS

- On December 24, 2002, Laci Peterson, who is eight months pregnant, disappears.
- Police question her husband, Scott Peterson, several times and note several discrepancies in his story.
- Amber Frey calls police on December 30, 2002, and informs them about her relationship with Scott.
- The remains of Laci Peterson and her child are found on April 13 and 14, 2003, not far from where Scott said he was fishing the day Laci vanished.
- Scott is arrested in April 2003 and charged with the murder of his wife and unborn child.
- Scott is convicted of murder and sentenced to death in 2004.
- After a long appeals process, Scott's death sentence is overturned in 2020 and he is resentenced to life in prison without the possibility of parole.
- In December 2022, a judge denies Scott a new trial based on the defense's allegation of juror misconduct.

KEY PLAYERS

- Laci Peterson, a young wife and mother-to-be, went missing on December 24, 2002.
- Scott Peterson, Laci Peterson's husband, was convicted of her murder and the murder of their unborn son largely on circumstantial evidence. He was sentenced to death, which was later reduced to life in prison without the possibility of parole.
- Amber Frey, a massage therapist, unknowingly began an affair with Scott Peterson in November 2002. After learning that he was married and a suspect in his wife's disappearance, she worked with the police to record her conversations with Scott.
- Detective Al Brocchini was a homicide detective in Modesto, California. Brocchini was one of the lead officers investigating the Peterson case.

IMPACT ON SOCIETY

In 2002, Laci Peterson made international headlines when the vibrant, young mother-to-be disappeared from her home without a trace. When massive search efforts yielded no significant leads, a shocking development emerged. Her husband, Scott, had been having an affair with a young woman named Amber Frey.

Though Laci's family and the public had steadfastly supported Scott in the early days of the investigation, the news of his infidelity shook their faith. Suddenly, many people began to look at Scott with suspicion. Although little physical evidence was found to link Scott to Laci's murder, he was eventually convicted and sentenced to death. Years later, Scott's death sentence was overturned and he was resentenced to life in prison without the possibility of parole.

QUOTE

"The family and friends of Laci have endured what only those who have lost someone to an act of senseless murder can ever begin to know. It has taken 20 years to reach this point . . . [and] not a day has gone by that Laci's family and friends have not thought of her and Conner and missed them with all their hearts. We as a community share in their loss."

—Stanislaus County District Attorney's Office

GLOSSARY

affair
A romantic or sexual relationship between two people when one or both parties are already in a committed relationship with someone else.

arraignment
A defendant's first court appearance, in which a judge formally announces a person's charges.

autopsy
An examination of a dead body to determine the cause of death.

canine
A dog or related to a dog.

circumstantial evidence
Evidence that does not directly prove a fact but can be used to support a theory.

coroner
An official who investigates suspicious, violent, or sudden deaths.

cross-examination
When a witness is questioned by an opposing side in a court of law.

decomposition
Decay caused by natural factors.

eulogy
A speech or piece of writing created to commemorate someone who is deceased.

felony
A serious crime, often involving violence.

fetus
An unborn baby.

forensic
Characterized by the use of scientific techniques to investigate a crime.

gestational age
A measurement of a fetus's age, calculated from the date of the mother's last menstrual cycle.

homicide
The killing of one person by another.

marina
A harbor with places for small boats and other watercraft.

maternity
Relating to something designed for pregnant people.

ornamental horticulture
The art or practice of garden cultivation and management.

polygraph test
A test that measures the body's physical response when being questioned. Police may interpret the results as proof of whether the person being questioned is lying.

surveillance
Close observation.

testimony
A formal or written statement often given in a court of law.

wiretap
A listening device used to conduct surveillance, typically over a phone line.

ADDITIONAL RESOURCES

SELECTED BIBLIOGRAPHY

Crier, Catherine. *A Deadly Game: The Untold Story of the Scott Peterson Investigation*. HarperCollins, 2005.

Frey, Amber. *Witness for the Prosecution of Scott Peterson*. Regan Books, 2005.

Rocha, Sharon. *For Laci: A Mother's Story of Love, Loss, and Justice*. Crown, 2006.

FURTHER READINGS

Cooper, Chris. *Forensic Science*. DK Publishing, 2020.

Lombardo, Jennifer. *Abusive Relationships and Domestic Violence*. Lucent Press, 2019.

Mooney, Carla. *The Watts Family Murders*. Abdo, 2024.

ONLINE RESOURCES

Booklinks
NONFICTION NETWORK
FREE! ONLINE NONFICTION RESOURCES

To learn more about preventing and investigating crimes, please visit **abdobooklinks.com** or scan this QR code. These links are routinely monitored and updated to provide the most current information available.

MORE INFORMATION

For more information on this subject, contact or visit the following organizations:

ALCATRAZ EAST CRIME MUSEUM

2757 Pkwy.
Pigeon Forge, TN 37863
alcatrazeast.com

The Alcatraz East Crime Museum offers information about forensic science and famous cases, such as the murder of Laci Peterson.

AMERICAN ACADEMY OF FORENSIC SCIENCES (AAFS)

410 N. 21st St.
Colorado Springs, CO 80904
aafs.org

The AAFS is a professional society dedicated to promoting forensic science education and improving accuracy and precision in forensic science.

SAN QUENTIN STATE PRISON

Main St.
San Quentin, CA 94964
cdcr.ca.gov/facility-locator/sq/

The San Quentin State Prison website offers information about the facility, its inmate population, and the death penalty in California.

SOURCE NOTES

CHAPTER 1. MISSING

1. Catherine Crier. *A Deadly Game: The Untold Story of the Scott Peterson Investigation.* HarperCollins, 2005. 6.

2. "Modesto, California." *Citytowninfo.com*, n.d., citytowninfo.com. Accessed 15 June 2023.

3. Crier, *Deadly Game*, 6–7.

4. "County and City Data Book: 2000." *United States Census Bureau*, 30 Sept. 2015, census.gov. Accessed 15 June 2023.

5. Crier, *Deadly Game*, 17–24.

6. "The Peterson Case: How They Got Scott," *People*, 23 May 2005, people.com. Accessed 15 June 2023.

CHAPTER 2. SCOTT AND LACI

1. "The Woman behind the Smile." *Modesto Bee*, 19 Apr. 2003, modbee.com. Accessed 15 June 2023.

2. Kelly St. John. "A Portrait of the Accused." *San Francisco Chronicle*, 7 Mar. 2004, sfgate.com. Accessed 15 June 2023.

3. St. John, "Portrait of the Accused."

4. St. John, "Portrait of the Accused."

5. Catherine Crier. *A Deadly Game: The Untold Story of the Scott Peterson Investigation.* HarperCollins, 2005. 59–60.

6. Crier, *Deadly Game*, 63–64.

7. Crier, *Deadly Game*, 62.

8. Crier, *Deadly Game*, 67.

CHAPTER 3. A MASSIVE SEARCH

1. "The Laci Peterson Story: A Dateline Investigation." *Dateline NBC*, season 25, episode 29, NBC, 22 Apr. 2017.

2. "The Peterson Case: How They Got Scott." *People*, 23 May 2005, people.com. Accessed 15 June 2023.

3. Janine DeFao. "Search On for Missing Modesto Woman." *San Francisco Chronicle*, 27 Dec. 2002, sfgate.com. Accessed 15 June 2023.

4. Doug Ridenour. "Search Continues for Missing Woman." *Modesto Police Department*, 26 Dec. 2002, pwc-sii.com. Accessed 15 June 2023.

5. "Police: Woman 'Did Not Walk Away Voluntarily.'" *CNN*, 1 Jan. 2003, cnn.com. Accessed 15 June 2023.

6. "Laci Peterson Story."

7. "Laci Peterson Story."

8. Catherine Crier. *A Deadly Game: The Untold Story of the Scott Peterson Investigation.* HarperCollins, 2005. 81–82.

9. Crier, *Deadly Game*, 96.

10. Crier, *Deadly Game*, 97.

11. Crier, *Deadly Game*, 100–101.

CHAPTER 4. SUSPICIONS RISE

1. Nicole Pelletiere. "Amber Frey Remembers Recorded Calls with Scott Peterson: 'I Was Shaking.'" *ABC News*, 14 Sept. 2017, abcnews.go.com. Accessed 15 June 2023.

2. "The Story of Scott and Amber." *CBS News*, 10 Aug. 2004, cbsnews.com. Accessed 15 June 2023.

3. "Story of Scott and Amber."

4. Matt Lauer. "Amber Frey Unravels Scott Peterson's Lies." *NBC News*, 4 Jan. 2005, nbcnews.com. Accessed 15 June 2023.

5. Pelletiere, "Recorded Calls with Scott Peterson."

6. "Peterson Admitted Lying to His Mistress." *NBC News*, 10 Aug. 2004, nbcnews.com. Accessed 15 June 2023.

7. "Peterson Admitted Lying to His Mistress."

8. Catherine Crier. *A Deadly Game: The Untold Story of the Scott Peterson Investigation.* HarperCollins, 2005. 214.

9. Crier, *Deadly Game*, 222.

10. Katie Couric. "For the Love of Laci." *NBC News*, 8 Jan. 2006, nbcnews.com. Accessed 15 June 2023.

11. Stacy Finz. "Scott Peterson Admits Affair, Denies Killing Pregnant Wife: He Says Laci, Modesto Police Knew about Other Woman." *San Francisco Chronicle*, 29 Jan. 2003, sfgate.com. Accessed 15 June 2023.

12. Jim Wasserman. "Police Classify Disappearance as Homicide." *Midland Daily News*, 3 Mar. 2003, ourmidland.com. Accessed 15 June 2023.

CHAPTER 5. DISCOVERY AND ARREST

1. Henry K. Lee and Meredith May. "Bodies of Fetus, Woman Found by Bay: Cops Investigating Laci Peterson Case Summoned to Site." *San Francisco Chronicle*, 15 Apr. 2003, sfgate.com. Accessed 15 June 2023.

2. Catherine Crier. *A Deadly Game: The Untold Story of the Scott Peterson Investigation.* HarperCollins, 2005. 337–338.

3. Crier, *Deadly Game*, 348.

4. Dave Jones. "Scott Peterson Arrested." *Modesto Bee*, 20 Nov. 2007, modbee.com. Accessed 15 June 2023.

5. Jones, "Scott Peterson Arrested."

6. Nick Madigan. "As Both Families Look On, Scott Peterson Denies Guilt." *New York Times*, 22 Apr. 2003, nytimes.com. Accessed 15 June 2023.

SOURCE NOTES CONTINUED

CHAPTER 6. THE TRIAL OF SCOTT PETERSON

1. "Laci Peterson Case: Prosecutor Points to Circumstantial Evidence." *CNN*, 2004, cnn.com. Accessed 15 June 2023.

2. "Laci Peterson Case: Defense: Two-Timer, Yes, but No Murderer." *CNN*, 31 Dec. 2007, cnn.com. Accessed 15 June 2023.

3. Jason Dearen. "Defense: Leads Ignored in Peterson Case." *East Bay Times*, 29 Sept. 2004, eastbaytimes.com. Accessed 15 June 2023.

4. Bryan Robinson. "Peterson Prosecution Gets Mixed Reviews." *ABC News*, 7 Oct. 2004, abcnews.go.com. Accessed 15 June 2023.

5. Bill Hewitt and Jill Smolowe. "Trapped on Tape?" *People*, 30 Aug. 2004, people.com. Accessed 15 June 2023.

6. Hewitt and Smolowe, "Trapped on Tape?"

7. Hewitt and Smolowe, "Trapped on Tape?"

8. Hewitt and Smolowe, "Trapped on Tape?"

9. Bryan Robinson. "Peterson Defense Faces Emotional Hurdle." *ABC News*, 11 Oct. 2004, abcnews.go.com. Accessed 15 June 2023.

10. "Defense Rests in Peterson Case." *NBC News*, 25 Oct. 2004, nbcnews.com. Accessed 15 June 2023.

11. "Defense Rests in Peterson Case."

12. Carolyn Marshall. "Prosecutor Tells Jury Peterson Killed Wife to Live a Fantasy." *New York Times*, 2 Nov. 2004, nytimes.com. Accessed 15 June 2023.

13. Carolyn Marshall. "Judge Dismisses Foreman from Peterson Jury." *New York Times*, 11 Nov. 2004, nytimes.com. Accessed 15 June 2023.

CHAPTER 7. GUILTY OF MURDER

1. "Laci Peterson Case: Jurors Find Scott Peterson Guilty of Murder." *CNN*, 2004, cnn.com. Accessed 15 June 2023.

2. Peter Aitken. "Scott Peterson Wasn't Expecting 'Guilty' Verdict in Murder of Wife Laci and Unborn Son." *Fox News*, 15 May 2021, foxnews.com. Accessed 15 June 2023.

3. John Coté. "Guilty: Jury Next to Decide If He'll Be Executed." *Modesto Bee*, 20 Nov. 2007, modbee.com. Accessed 15 June 2023.

4. Carolyn Marshall. "Jury Finds Scott Peterson Guilty of Wife's Murder." *New York Times*, 13 Nov. 2004, nytimes.com. Accessed 15 June 2023.

5. Dean Murphy. "Scott Peterson Sentenced to Death for Killing Pregnant Wife." *New York Times*, 10 Dec. 2004, nytimes.com. Accessed 15 June 2023.

6. Coté, "Guilty: Jury Next to Decide If He'll Be Executed."

7. Catherine Crier. *A Deadly Game: The Untold Story of the Scott Peterson Investigation.* HarperCollins, 2005. 414–417.

8. Crier, *Deadly Game*, 419.

9. Dean Murphy. "'Divorce Was an Option,' Laci Peterson's Mother Cries." *New York Times*, 1 Dec. 2004, nytimes.com. Accessed 15 June 2023.

10. "Laci Peterson Life Insurance Goes to Mother." *NBC News*, 21 Oct. 2004, nbcnews.com. Accessed 15 June 2023.

11. Crier, *Deadly Game*, 4.

12. Dean Murphy. "Scott Peterson's Mother Pleads with Jurors for a Life Sentence." *New York Times*, 9 Dec. 2004, nytimes.com. Accessed 15 June 2023.

13. Dean Murphy. "Jury Begins Deliberating Scott Peterson's Punishment." *New York Times*, 10 Dec. 2004, nytimes.com. Accessed 15 June 2023.

14. Murphy, "Scott Peterson Sentenced to Death for Killing Pregnant Wife."

CHAPTER 8. YEARS OF APPEALS

1. "San Quentin Doors Clang Shut behind Peterson." *NBC News*, 17 Mar. 2005, nbcnews.com. Accessed 15 June 2023.

2. "San Quentin State Prison (SQ)." *California Department of Corrections and Rehabilitation*, n.d., cdcr.ca.gov. Accessed 15 June 2023.

3. Paul Elias. "Scott Peterson Appeals Death Sentence." *Orange County Register*, 6 July 2012, ocregister.com. Accessed 15 June 2023.

4. Elias, "Scott Peterson Appeals Death Sentence."

5. Jenny Gross. "Scott Peterson's Death Sentence Is Overturned." *New York Times*, 24 Aug. 2020, nytimes.com. Accessed 15 June 2023.

6. "California Governor Announces Moratorium on Executions." *Death Penalty Information Center*, 13 Mar. 2019, deathpenaltyinfo.org. Accessed 15 June 2023.

7. "Scott Peterson Death Penalty Overturned by California Supreme Court." *NBC News*, 24 Aug. 2020, nbcnews.com. Accessed 15 June 2023.

8. Mimi Dwyer. "California Court Ordered to Reconsider Scott Peterson Murder Conviction." *Reuters*, 15 Oct. 2020, reuters.com. Accessed 15 June 2023.

9. Erin Tracy. "Update: Here's How the Judge Made Her Decision to Deny Scott Peterson a New Trial." *Modesto Bee*, 20 Dec. 2022, modbee.com. Accessed 15 June 2023.

10. "California Prosecutors Again Seek Death for Scott Peterson." *US News*, 24 Oct. 2020, usnews.com. Accessed 15 June 2023.

11. Stephanie Pagones. "Scott Peterson Loses New Trial Bid; Convicted Killer to Remain behind Bars." *Fox News*, 20 Dec. 2020, foxnews.com. Accessed 15 June 2023.

12. Jill Sederstrom. "Laci Peterson's Family Relieved Scott Peterson Won't Get New Trial." *Yahoo Money*, 22 Dec. 2022, money.yahoo.com. Accessed 15 June 2023.

INDEX

ABOUT THE AUTHOR

CARLA MOONEY

Carla Mooney is a graduate of the University of Pennsylvania. Today, she writes for young people and is the author of many books for young adults and children. Mooney enjoys reading about true crime and forensic investigations.